norman's ark

norman's ark

By Thelma Norman

Cover and illustrations by
Ralph McDonald

Southern Publishing Association
Nashville, Tennessee

This book was
Edited by Gerald Wheeler
Designed by Dean Tucker

Text set in 12/13 Fairfield
Printed on Pinnacle Book Offset
    Antique
Cover stock: Springhill Gloss
    Bristol

Printed in U.S.A.

contents

7/The Perils and Pleasures of Zoo Keeping

14/Pitty-pat and Flanagan

24/Butch

34/Pretty Girl.

43/André

50/Fuffy

62/Mick

71/"THAT COATI!"

77/Little Jag and Skee

86/Mud and Ape

95/T-Bird

104/Sugar and Eagle

111/Cookie

117/Horses, Horses, Horses!

126/Nip 'n' Tuck

130/The Lettuce Eaters

137/Tiki

152/Cold-blooded Crawling Things

The Perils and Pleasures of Zoo Keeping

R-r-ring!

The telephone shrills through a house that is neither empty nor quiet, even though I am the only person home. I disentangle T-Bird's arms from around my neck and unceremoniously deposit him on the arm of the sofa as I rise to answer the summoning bell. T-Bird, a baby woolly monkey, has a yen for playing with the telephone at the same time I'm trying to use it.

I pick up the receiver after the fifth or sixth ring, about par for the course, and answer, "Hello!"

"Is this the Norman residence?"

"Ye——" I intended to say, "Yes, it is. This is Mrs. Norman!" but Butch, the myna bird, shouts from his perch beside the telephone, "Hello! Hello!" and drowns out all I'm trying to say.

And the caller once more says, "Hello?" in a tentative, questioning tone.

"This is Mrs.——" I try once more, but "THAT COATI!," our coatimundi, climbs up my arm and sniffs loudly into the phone.

"Is anything wrong?" inquires the lady on the other end of the line.

"No, really! It's just——" I hesitate as Skee, with a spit and a swat of his paw, drives "THAT COATI!" away and leaps to my shoulder. "My cat just jumped up onto my shoulder and startled me," I manage to say at last.

"Oh-h-h, you have a kitten," she coos. "I just love a cuddly little kitten."

"Uh—yes, we do have a cat," I reply, wondering what she'd say if I told her my "kitten" was a full-grown South American wildcat.

"But this *is* the Norman residence, isn't it? I'm trying to locate the doctor."

"The doctor is working late at the office this evening," I reply briskly. "You can reach him there."

After such a conversation I am apt to sit musing a bit. "Is this the Norman residence?" I answer that question affirmatively every day, but sometimes, after a glance at the zoo in my living room, I'm tempted to say instead, "This is Normans' ark!"

In a home where animals and people mix in unequal

8

proportions, with the people in the minority, the unexpected is no longer surprising and things are not always what they seem.

The people are not the only ones who talk—the two myna birds, Butch and George, sometimes carry on surprisingly coherent conversations, as well as mimic the other animals. The canary chirps and whistles, but so does the jaguarundi cat, Skee, though he doesn't meow. Mick, a dingy black poodle, keeps order among the other animals with an astonishing sense of fair play. The monkey refuses to eat monkey pellets, but the coatimundi devours them with gusto. Bib, a mongrel dog whose only pedigree is a long history of loyalty and devotion, gently takes the hem of my skirt in his mouth and leads me where he thinks I should go. These, and others, make up my zoo that overflows from the house into the yard, garage, and barn. The population fluctuates, as some animals remain in residence only until we can find another home for them.

I never meant to have a zoo, even on so small a scale as this. In fact, I never even saw a zoo until I was old enough to vote, but I always loved animals. At home, while I grew up, we frequently had young wild animals and birds my father had found abandoned or orphaned and had brought home for us to raise. It seemed natural to me for animals and people to share a home. But in the beginning, I never intended to have as many animals as I ended up with. I started out with the usual cat, dog, and canary. My family and friends who knew my fondness for animals gave me the others, or I bought them as gifts for my children, who would rather have animals for birthdays and Christmas presents than anything else. Once in a while (I whisper it softly) I even bought one for myself.

Of course any venture of this sort has inherent problems.

Elementary is the fact that the animals must eat. So far it has not been a serious matter, except for finding myself out of animal food after the stores have closed for a weekend or holiday. All of the animals I've had have eaten foods commonly available. I have to specially order the monkey pellets, but they come within a few days, and I always keep an extra sack of them on hand.

Far harder than finding the proper diet for my animals is keeping them from getting food that isn't good for them. It is a difficult thing to keep visitors from giving T-Bird more candy than he should have, because he so obviously enjoys it and begs so sweetly for it. "THAT COATI!"'s way of eating watermelon is so comical that I have to firmly restrict the amount given him. Mick will do his tricks endlessly for cookies, and the children would give the horses a whole box of sugar cubes in one afternoon just to feel the animals' velvety noses on the palms of their hands as they pick the cubes up. Young visitors shout with laughter to see Skee dance on his legs begging for a taste of *anything* that comes out of a can, although he refuses to eat anything that isn't cat food, so that isn't really much of a problem. Skee's dietary problem is that he'd love to sample the myna birds and the canary. For live food he has to content himself with an occasional mouse he catches himself.

Housing is something else to consider when dealing with animals. Even though all our indoor pets, except the birds, have the run of the house at least part of the day, most of them need cages for sleeping. We clean the cages once or twice daily, making it necessary to keep bales of old newspapers on hand. Whenever an animal is out of his cage, we leave the door open so that he can have quick and easy access to his sanctuary if he's frightened. Most of them respect the others' cages as their castles and stay out of them.

Sometimes factors beyond my control precipitate a situation that endangers my animals, such as the winter night the thermostat on the furnace broke down. When the cold awakened me, I realized that while most of the animals would likely be all right, the myna birds could easily develop respiratory trouble and die from it. We had electric blankets in the house, so we put them over the birdcages, keeping close watch over the temperature to see that the birds didn't get too warm. In a matter of hours we got the thermostat repaired, and the birds emerged with no ill effects.

A potentially more dangerous predicament occurred the night our electric lines went down during a small blizzard. My husband was at the hospital with a critically ill patient, so I had to cope with my problem single-handedly. This time even the electric blankets were of no use. We piled all our extra blankets over the bird and animal cages and hoped for the best. As soon as it was daylight, I warmed up my station wagon and put the birds in the front seat. With the children in the middle seat and the animals in the back, I started to my husband's office, which the blackout had not affected. It was not an easy trip, for it was still snowing, visibility was poor, and we encountered several nearly impassable drifts.

When I reached the clinic and settled children and pets in the warm basement, I had a hard time convincing anyone I had driven in. The Safety Patrol had advised people not to try to travel our road, saying it had drifted shut since midnight. Fortunately, I had not known the fact and had made the trip, if not easily, at least successfully. Several hours later repair crews had put the lines back in operation, and we returned home down the road the Safety Patrol still insisted was blocked. I made my last trip of that day just before midnight, going to bring my husband home because his car couldn't negotiate the drifts; and shortly after we got home, the road really did blow shut. We remained snow-bound for two days.

Despite all one can do, pets, like people, become ill. Unlike people, a pet can't say, "I hurt here and here, and the pain is dull and throbbing." Sometimes, when I place a hurried call to our family veterinarian, I can more easily empathize with the frantic calls that come to my husband at all hours of the day and night. Next to food and shelter, the best thing a pet owner can provide for his animal is a good veterinarian.

If by now I've given you the impression that owning pets is nothing but one trouble after another, let me remove that notion. I merely listed the liabilities first to get them out of the way quickly so that I could get down to something I really love to talk about—the joys of having pets.

I own pets because I love animals. That in itself provides enough excuse to justify having them in my home. But it isn't the only reason.

I have pets because I want my children to love and enjoy them, too. I believe that a child who has a healthy love for animals will be kind to his fellowmen. And I want my children to grow up with a feeling of compassion for those more helpless and weaker than they. Caring for animals is a good way to encourage the early development of such an attitude.

I have pets because I learn from them. Although I am not an expert in animal behavior or anything else pertaining to animals and cannot speak with authority on any except those I have owned, I have learned from each one of them, directly or indirectly.

I have pets because they provide me with companionship while my husband is working and the children are at school. When T-Bird nestles on one shoulder with his arms around my neck, "THAT COATI!" cuddles in my lap, and Skee curls up purring against the other shoulder, each happy and contented, I get a faint glimpse of Eden, where man and all animals lived at peace with one another, and I dream of a heavenly home where it will be that way again.

I have pets because through them I can bring pleasure to others. Few children are indifferent to animals, and so my pets and I frequently visit Vacation Bible Schools, summer camps, and youth meetings. When T-Bird pats a child's face and the child squeals in delight, "He touched me! He reached right out and touched me!" I feel that child's delight. When "THAT COATI!" sniffs at a shy little hand near the bars of his cage and the owner of the hand looks up in wonder and says, "Oh, his nose is so soft!" I feel that wonder. Through the eyes of the children I see and appreciate my pets anew. And should they draw the children closer to their heavenly Father, who loved us and created the animals for our pleasure, that is the best reason of all for having pets.

If, as you read the following chapters, you feel that I've ascribed too-human traits to my animals, I offer no apologies, for I wrote about them just as they seemed to be to me. For who has not, at some time or other, said or heard someone else say about a cherished dog, "He's so nearly human we sometimes forget he's a dog"? And maybe my pets sometimes think about me, "She's so like us we forget she is a human." If so, I think they'd mean it as a compliment.

Pitty-pat and Flanagan

We had been dogless for months, ever since we had moved into a new neighborhood. Baby, our black cocker, let us know that he much preferred his old home by running back to it every time he got loose. He ran away despite the fact that our new yard contained countless trees and bushes to investigate, all kinds of birds to watch and chase, squirrels to torment, and even a lily pond to drink from; and the house was large, with many nooks and crannies to explore.

All this, however, paled beside the lure of the familiar. We had to face the humiliating fact that it was not the family but the old homestead to which he gave his loyalty, and after numerous trips to bring him home, we finally gave him to our former neighbor, with whom he had taken up residence.

Now, as I said, we were without a dog, but it was not a state we could allow to exist for long. Early one spring morning I took the children in the car, and we drove off to the local animal shelter to find a pet.

Each one of the children had his own ideas about the kind of dog we should get. Ray wanted a German shepherd, Gigi desired a collie, Jimmy wished for another cocker, and Danny Joe could only shout, "Puppy, Mamma! Doggie! Get a doggie!" My own choice, I knew, would depend on what was available.

By the time we reached the animal shelter, the children had risen to such a state of excitement that I had to leave them in the car, a highly unpopular decision, for not one of them felt that he could trust me to get the kind of dog he asked for. I promised them that once I'd chosen "our" dog, I'd let them come in and see the others *if* they had behaved themselves in the meantime.

Inside, an attendant showed me a pen full of dogs waiting for new homes. Two adorable fox terrier puppies caught my eye immediately, but when I began to question the attendant, he said, "Sorry, ma'am, somebody has already spoken for those two dogs. All the others are available, though."

I looked around at the rest of the dogs in the pen. Mentally I crossed off all the big dogs, even though two of the children had asked for a German shepherd or a collie. That still left a large number to choose from. They included sev-

15

eral dogs that I thought were beagles, a sprightly cocker or two, a small dog at least part rat terrier that looked scared of her own shadow, and many others whose mixed ancestry I could not identify with any certainty.

I didn't want an overly aggressive dog, and I certainly did not want the poor slinking terrier that would probably die of heart failure if someone spoke to her. What I wanted was a friendly, inquisitive small dog.

Some of the dogs bounded to the fence immediately and tried to reach my hands. Those, I'd been warned, were the ones who might prove too exuberant later. Others were more cautious but did come over to make friendly overtures. From that group I decided to choose my dog. The little brown and white terrier never made a move.

My husband had owned a rat terrier during his youth. She died while he served in the military overseas. Perhaps his often-mentioned Peggy had looked like the one before me, but from what I'd heard of Peggy's liveliness, looks were all the two dogs had in common. I felt it would be too big a chance to take the frightened part terrier home and hope that love would perform a miracle for her.

Carefully I surveyed the group of eligibles. One looked part Manchester. Perhaps he would do. And did that one over there have a bit of spitz in him? I'd had a toy spitz puppy when I was a little girl, and I knew how lovable it could be.

The attendant stopped by while I debated the merits of the two dogs. "Well, ma'am," he said, "have you picked out a dog?"

"Yes," I replied, coming to a sudden decision. "I want that brown and white terrier over there."

He looked surprised, voiced his mild disapproval, and brought her to me. While we went through the formalities that made her mine, she trembled, and I could feel her heart thumping wildly.

My own heart almost failed me as I went out the door. If she appeared so frightened of me, how would she react to the carful of children, and what would they think of her?

Danny Joe saw us first. Leaning perilously far out the car window, he called out, "That my doggie! I love he! Leave he alone!" He addressed the last remark to the other children, who had also caught sight of us by now.

A clamor of remarks now arose. "Oh, look! Isn't she cute?" "May I hold her, Mom?" "No, me!" "I asked first, Mom." "What's its name?" "I love he. He my dog!"

Holding the shivering dog close, I explained to the children that she was frightened and that they must act extremely gentle with her. It took a great effort on their part, but they did become quiet and began to pet the dog now huddled on the seat beside them. Her confidence grew, and her fear melted under the influence of their petting. Finally she ventured a tentative caress with her rough little tongue, followed by a heart-stopping pause as she waited to see how we would receive it. Finding that it brought only more loving pats and words, she launched herself upon the children, licking them ecstatically and wagging her tail as if her small body could not express the happiness now coursing through it.

Finally, in a momentary pause, I asked, "Do you want to go in now and see the others?"

"No, no! Let's take her home right now so we can play with her."

After their unanimous request, I started the car and away we went. Within a few minutes the little terrier had her nose out the car window, barking at every car we met. What was she trying to say? I wondered. Perhaps she was proclaiming, "Look at me, everybody. See, I'm loved! I belong to someone. Look at me!" Or perhaps she was announcing, "Listen to me! This is my family, and if you harm a one of them, you'll have me to deal with."

When we arrived home, I watched as children and dog romped on the lawn, feeling sure the attendant at the animal shelter would no longer recognize the poor frightened dog he'd handed to me such a short time before. With her ears pricked up alertly, her eyes shining, her tail wagging so fast that it looked almost a blur, she ran and rolled on the grass with the children. Love *had* worked its miracle.

When the children took her inside to acquaint her with the house, I listened to her pattering feet as they went from room to room, and a name for the little waif popped into my mind. Therefore, when a few minutes later one of the children asked, "What shall we call her?" I answered, "Let's call her Pitty-pat. Doesn't that fit her?"

One of my children, with greater perception than I'd given him credit for, cried out in glee, "That's what her feet say when she runs on the linoleum."

She came obediently whenever anyone called her name. Surely sometime or other she'd had another name. Her fear at the animal shelter had not been that of a habitually mistreated animal, but rather the bewilderment of one separated from those she loved for no reason she could understand. I could imagine the sadness of her former owners as circumstances forced them to leave her at the shelter, where they could only hope someone would see her and give her a home. I longed to let them know that we loved her and would care for her, but I knew the rules forbade the giving of any information to either her former owners or to us.

"Well, look who's here!" My husband smiled when Pitty-pat greeted him on his return home. He knelt to pet her, then looked up to say, "She reminds me a lot of Peggy."

"We've been calling her Pitty-pat, but we can rename her Peggy if you like," I replied.

"No," he said thoughtfully. "I think Pitty-pat just suits her." Then as he held her on his lap and stroked her, we told him the story of how we had gotten her at the animal shelter.

Later we made her a bed in a large upstairs closet, and she settled comfortably for the night.

It seemed that every succeeding day we found something more to love and appreciate in our new pet. Inside the house she displayed an attitude of quiet decorum that would explode into vibrant playfulness as she romped outside with the children.

One of my friends once exclaimed about her, "Pitty-pat is every inch a lady. She could give some people I know lessons in courtesy."

Each morning I would let her outside, and she would wander around the neighborhood on business of her own. When I returned home from taking the older children to school, she would sit waiting to come inside. It was as if she thought I needed her companionship during the hours the children were gone. She had a favorite spot in each room where she settled herself while I remained in that room. If I sat down, she would lie down beside my chair.

She made it a point to greet every guest who entered our house, without forcing her attentions upon them. Her playing with little children showed her great patience. At times she must have tolerated an inordinate amount of ear tugging, nose punching, whisker pulling, and stomach thumping from young visitors before I noticed her predicament and rescued her, but I have never once heard her complain.

One morning the children raced downstairs with the

19

news that Pitty-pat had two puppies, something we had partially expected. I cautioned the children against picking up the tiny babies, explaining that it wouldn't be good for them and that it would upset Pitty-pat. They spent as much time as they could watching the puppies.

The puppies grew and thrived. Both were females, and I hoped they'd have their mother's disposition, even though both of them looked much like their Boston terrier father. The children pleaded so hard to keep them that I at length weakened and said we'd keep *one* if daddy agreed.

The children discussed the situation among themselves, and I never knew exactly how they decided which puppy they wanted. After they made their decision, they put the question to their father when he came home from the clinic.

"Daddy, may we keep one of the puppies? Please, Daddy?"

"Wel-l-l-l," he hesitated, and lost the battle.

"Oh, thank you, Daddy, thank you!" four happy voices exclaimed.

"But only one puppy, you understand," daddy said firmly, trying to salvage some semblance of his parental authority.

"We know just which one we want to keep," they chorused, and ran to get the chosen one to show him. Pitty-pat had weaned them by then, and within a day or so we had placed the other pup in a good home.

When the children began wanting a name for the remaining puppy, I told them I'd try to think of a suitable one. For several days I thought it over, but nothing appropriate came to mind. One day, tired of the constant request "What are we going to name the puppy, Mamma?" I answered, "We're going to call her Flanagan." It was a remark I regretted many times in subsequent weeks. When people would ask the children why they named the pup Flanagan, they would say, "You had better ask mamma. She named it." Then when the questioner came to me, I could only explain somewhat lamely that it was the only name I could think of for her. Flanagan, as I'd hoped, had her mother's personality, which only made her ridiculous name more incongruous.

When Flanagan was about five months old, she awakened us one night by her whimpering and crying. Pitty-pat walked about nervously as we tried to find out the problem. The young dog's whining and crying continued at intervals until we took her to the animal hospital the next day about noon.

The doctor was out, but his young assistant took Flanagan and listened to our story. Smilingly he told us that he didn't feel that Flanagan was sick; probably she just wanted attention. However, he agreed to keep her at the hospital for the doctor to see, and we'd hear from him later that afternoon.

Within a short time the doctor called us. Flanagan, he said, had Saint Vitus's dance, a serious malady in dogs. He could treat her, but the process would be long and expensive, with small chance of her recovery. And if she did get through the acute stage, she might be in almost constant pain for the rest of her life. Although the final decision was up to us, he felt that, gloomy as the prognosis was, the kindest thing would be to put her to sleep. Reluctantly we agreed, and we shed many tears over the results of that hard choice.

Pitty-pat grieved over the loss of her little daughter and playmate. We tried to give her extra love and attention. She recovered her spirits in a short time, but she never again slept in the large closet she and Flanagan had shared. Instead, she spent the night under the living-room couch.

Two years went by, and there came a spring that was

one of the loveliest that I could ever remember. Rain seemed to fall at exactly the right time, and the flowers bloomed spectacularly.

One day when my husband came home for lunch, I walked out to the car with him. We stopped to admire the spirea and lilacs in bloom. Spying Pitty-pat resting in the shade of a tree in the corner of the yard by the driveway, I called to her. She raised her head and looked, but didn't come—something so unusual that I walked down to where she lay. When I got close, I stopped in horror. A car had hit her and almost torn her right front leg off. We had no way of knowing how long she'd waited there for help to come. Neither could we tell if the accident had happened right there, or if she'd dragged herself home after getting hit somewhere else.

My shocked outcry brought my husband running. He took charge immediately. "I'll bring the car down while you get a blanket. We'll take her right up to the clinic," he ordered. But when Pitty-pat saw both of us move away, she made a pitiful effort to follow, so I called that I'd stay with her. He could bring both the blanket and the car. I sat beside her, patting and rubbing her, assuring her that we'd have her taken care of in no time at all. I wasn't nearly as confident as I tried to sound, though. My presence comforted her, and while I know it must have been exceedingly painful to her, she made no protest of any kind when we transferred her to the car.

At the clinic we put her on the X-ray table, and while the patients in the waiting room wondered what delayed their afternoon appointments, we examined her more closely.

"That leg is just hanging by a flap of skin," my husband said. "I'm going to remove it and try to close the wound. I believe there's enough skin to cover it. There seem to be no other injuries. If she stands the shock of this bit of surgery, she might pull through."

When he began to close the wound, the pain must have been agonizing, for Pitty-pat suddenly bared her teeth and snarled at him. Then immediately, with a sobbing little whimper, she began to lick his hand and her eyes begged him to forgive her. I turned away in tears, and one of the nurses walked quickly into the X-ray darkroom, while the other one stood wiping her eyes. I realized that my husband controlled himself only with an effort as he continued the suturing up, but by the time he finished, we were all more or less composed again.

Pitty-pat seemed no worse after the surgery, so I took her home and put her in a box in the living room. She was thirsty, and after drinking, she fell asleep. All through the night one or two of us kept watch over her, petting and encouraging her, bringing her water and propping her up with pillows to help her breathe easier. In spite of all we could do, she died early the next morning.

We buried her under a lilac bush in the yard where she had spent so many happy hours. The most fitting epitaph we could think of for her was the statement made by my friend, "She was every inch a lady."

Butch

My husband had told me that if I'd make out the income tax return that year, I could have any refund. Being quite confused by anything involving mathematics, I went down to the main post office, where a man helped me make out the papers. When we finished, he remarked casually, "Well, it looks as if you'll get a refund in the neighborhood of five hundred dollars." It seemed such an astronomical sum that I just didn't believe it, and when the check arrived, I was as surprised as if I'd never heard the amount mentioned before. My husband spoke wistfully of the bills that money would pay, so I gave it to him, keeping only a small part for myself.

I knew exactly what I wanted to buy with my part, though. But by the time I had called on every pet store in town and they had told me that the pet I wanted wouldn't be available for several months, I was nearly frantic, for I knew my money wouldn't be available in several months—it would have melted away as money has a habit of doing.

My last hope, and a fragile one it was, centered around the Want Ad section of our newspaper. The first thing that met my eyes under the heading of "Pets" was a big ad:

"Closeout Sale.
Ella, the Bird Lady.
Parrots, Canaries, Myna Birds,
Cockatoos, Parrakeets, Cockatiels.
Greatly Reduced Prices!"

I hurried to the telephone, and when the Bird Lady answered, I inquired breathlessly, "Do you have any myna birds left?"

She informed me that she had one and welcomed me to come and look at it if I wanted to. Within minutes I had driven there.

Butch was the first myna bird I'd ever seen, though I had dreamed for years of owning one, ever since I'd read about them in a nationally known magazine. A beautiful bird, his plumage was an iridescent black, and he had bright yellow flaps of bare skin, called wattles, that started just below his eyes and met at the back of his head. He had an engaging way of turning his head upside down to stare at me, but did not indicate whether I looked better from that angle or not.

Ella told me that Butch was the best myna bird she'd had, and she had saved him to sell last. She said she had suffered from bronchitis and arthritis all winter long and finally had to give up her bird business because she couldn't take care of it anymore.

I was ready to buy Butch right then, but the woman informed me that someone else had come to see about him before I arrived.

"It was a major from the air base," she said, "and I hate to sell Butch to him because he uses such bad language. I'll let you know in the morning what I decide."

So I went home bitterly disappointed, sure that the major would get the bird.

Ella did not leave me long in suspense, for she called early the next day. "Mrs. Norman," she said, "I've decided to let you have Butch. That major came out here, and you should have heard the language he used! I just didn't want a nice bird like Butch learning such things. And I told him so, too! He didn't like it one bit, but he had to accept it."

I found that her greatly reduced prices enabled me to buy both Butch and his cage. She gave me a list of words and phrases that comprised Butch's vocabulary and told me he'd have to get used to us before he'd talk when we were around. Next she described how to take care of him and how to feed him, and said to call her if I had any questions.

At home I put Butch's cage on the living-room table where he could see all that went on. I wanted him to get used to us and start talking in a hurry, but he said nothing all day. I didn't worry, for Ella had said it might take several days.

The next morning, just before daybreak, the sound of coughing awakened me. I got up to see which child had developed such a cold overnight, but not a child stirred. I went back to bed, but before I could get back to sleep, I heard the cough again. Again I checked the children and found them all sleeping peacefully. This time, as I crossed the hall to my own bedroom, I heard the cough once more. It came from Butch. He sounded as if he were ready to die of consumption.

I ran in to wake my husband.

"Do you know what?" I demanded of my sleep-groggy spouse. "That little old lady cheated us! She sold us a sick bird. Just listen to him cough."

Obligingly, Butch coughed again.

"See?" I said. "And she seemed such a nice old lady, too. I'll bet that bird doesn't live twenty-four hours."

My husband shook his head to clear it. "He does have a bad cough, doesn't he? Sounds like a terrible lung condition of some kind. It's funny, though—I never heard a sick bird cough before."

Lung condition? Could it be——? Ella had told me that she'd had bronchitis all winter. By now I realized what he was doing. Butch was only mimicking her cough. He wasn't sick at all.

I sheepishly explained the situation to my husband, who muttered something about having enough to do taking care of sick people without having to listen to birds that coughed, and then went back to sleep.

The next day Butch would talk if we happened to be in another room. Before long he exercised his vocabulary no matter which of the family was around. I noticed he was particularly talkative about midmorning and midafternoon. I'd hear a steady stream of chatter from him then.

I had done some reading on myna birds and learned that there are several kinds, not all of which talk. The best talkers, as far as I could discover, were the Greater Indian

Hill mynas. Since myna birds do not breed in captivity, the suppliers must get them from the wild. The natives watch for myna bird nests and take the young when they are only a few weeks old. After hand feeding them for a few more weeks, the suppliers ship the fledglings by air to pet shops all over the world.

Butch was fond of water and loved to bathe many times a day. After he had vigorously splashed table, floor, walls, and curtains a few times, I decided he could bathe in the bathtub the way the rest of us did. I'd put a couple of inches of tepid water in the tub and let him splash as much as he wanted. Whenever he'd hear me running water in the bathtub, he'd call, "Butch wants a bath! Butch wants a bath!"

Besides being the family clown, Butch was a good baby-sitter. Our youngest child was only six months old when we got Butch, and whenever he cried, we'd pull his crib over near the bird's cage. Butch would get down in the corner of his cage as close to the baby as possible, and coax, "Pretty boy. Do you like Butch? Hello, Sweetheart. Good boy, pretty boy." And within minutes the baby would stop crying.

Since an old woman had trained Butch, his voice sounded like hers at first. Later he picked up words and phrases from us, also the tones of our voices. He learned to call the children just as I did. A few times they did not come when I called, explaining that they thought it was Butch. I convinced them that it would be in their best interests to learn the difference, and they did.

One day I had an important engagement. At the last minute the baby-sitter could not come. The mother of one of my friends volunteered to watch the children for me. She'd never been in our home before, and I just had time to introduce her to the children and leave.

As she went through the house, she heard an old woman

demanding, "What *are* you doing?" Thinking there must be someone she hadn't met, she looked around but couldn't find anyone. The next time she heard the voice, the baby-sitter went to the children and questioned them about it. "Oh, that's just Butch," they told her. Puzzled, but thinking that if the children knew about it, it must be all right, she walked through the sun porch. As she passed through it, she glanced at Butch as he spoke again, and discovered the source of the haughty voice.

Sometimes Butch would mumble things we couldn't understand. One series of jumbled words ended, "And be sure to shut the door!" Another closed with "Be careful of the dog!"

Several times Butch used a word or phrase at a particularly apt time, and no amount of coaxing could get him to repeat it.

One day I went to scrub the sun porch. As I came into the room, my pan of warm soapy water slipped, and there I stood with water all over me. "Just look at that!" I said in exasperation. "I'm soaking wet!"

"Oh, that's too bad!" Butch said in a voice dripping with sympathy. I assume he took his cue from the tone of my voice, but we could never again get him to repeat his comment.

One day we came back from town to find Butch's cage open and him gone. Black myna bird feathers lay all over the floor. We knew then that our puppy had killed and eaten him. I went about in a blue fog for hours, thinking how much I'd miss Butch's chatter and companionship, his clowning and impudence.

About bedtime that evening, Jimmy called out, "Mamma, here's Butch way back under the couch."

"Is he—is he dead?" I hardly dared ask.

"No," he said, bringing out the poor bird. "He's all right, only he's lost some feathers."

Butch was glad to get back into his own cage, but his silence told us more than anything could have that he'd had a terrible experience. Three days went by, and Butch never said a word. A fourth day. We began to wonder if he would ever talk again. On the fifth day Butch spoke. Brief, expressive, and right to the point, he repeated one word over and over during the next few days: "Ouch!" I don't know where he learned it. He never used it again after that.

Butch made an awful mess with his food. Since he did not have a gizzard, he had to have food in front of him all the time. He would get a piece of banana or other soft fruit stuck to his beak, snap his head to get it off, and the food particles would fly, to land on the furniture or wall. We had to clean the floor of his cage twice a day and replenish his water just as often.

Raymond had charge of cleaning and caring for Butch. The year he started to academy he had to go to school an hour earlier than previously, and even though I woke him up earlier, he never seemed to get quite through before time to go to school.

One morning about ten o'clock Butch called me. "Mamma, come here. Come on, now, Mamma!"

I went to see what the trouble was, and found that Raymond had not given him any water. I spoke to Raymond about it, and he promised that it wouldn't happen again. For some time it didn't.

Then Butch began to call me again, and each time that he was so insistent, I discovered that he either had no food or no water. I puzzled over how to impress Raymond with the importance of doing his work thoroughly.

The next morning when we had gone about halfway to

school, I drove over to the side of the road and stopped. "You'll have to walk from here, Ray," I said.

"Why, is there something wrong with the car?" he asked.

"No," I replied. "You've been neglecting Butch again lately, and I decided that if you're going to do your work halfway, I'm only going to drive you halfway to school."

"But I'll be late," he protested.

"What happens then?"

"I'll have to stop at the principal's office. He will want to know why I'm late," Raymond said, "and I'll have to tell him." He paused, and I could tell he was imagining the scene and finding it not at all to his liking. "He will think it's funny and so will all the teachers—you only bringing me halfway to school because I didn't do all my work, I mean."

"I suppose maybe they will," I commented.

"Mom, if I promise, really promise, never to neglect Butch again, will you drive me the rest of the way to school?"

"This one time I will," I agreed, starting the car, "but the next time you forget, you'll have to walk all the way to school, the whole two and one-half miles."

"That won't happen," he said confidently—and it didn't.

But it wasn't the only time that year that Butch got Ray into trouble.

It dawned on me one day that whenever I came home from an errand in the afternoon, I'd almost always find a group of the academy boys playing tackle football with Raymond in our field. Always putting a stop to it, I insisted they play touch football instead, but I noticed the game always broke up shortly afterward, as if they had little interest in the touch version. Also I asked Raymond if he had called the boys to come over and play. He said he hadn't. I noticed, however, that the pattern continued.

31

One day I again talked to Raymond about it. "Ray, how is it that the boys come only when I'm gone?" I asked.

"Well, it just happens that way," he answered.

"That's too much coincidence to accept," I said. "I believe you call them."

"No, I don't," he insisted. "They just get together and come."

Then one day I had a call to make. The minute I picked up the phone, Butch spoke up from his perch nearby. "Hello," he said. "This is Raymond Norman calling. Can you come over?"

I didn't tell Ray what I'd heard. I just waited until Butch repeated his remark when we were both present.

"Why, you dumb tattletale——" Ray began angrily, but then he laughed as the humor of the situation struck him.

"Well?" I said.

"Oh, all right!" Ray admitted. "I did call them and then lied about it. I'm sorry, Mom. It was just because we couldn't play tackle football anywhere else. I won't do it again—I promise."

One summer one of the local department stores had some myna birds for sale, so I bought another one as company for Butch. We called the new bird George.

Although George never seemed to acquire the words Butch had already picked up, Butch learned every expression George knew. Then he either mangled them or improved on them by combining them with his own. George might say, "Where are you going?" Butch would turn it into, "Where is Raymond going?" If George said, "What are you doing?" Butch might change it to, "What is daddy doing?" He always had the tenses right, too.

Once in a while the two birds seemed to carry on a fairly intelligent conversation. One I heard went like this:

Butch: Dad!
George: What?
Butch: Come here.
George: Why?
Butch: Oh, shut up!

Once we decided to see if their vocabularies would increase if we separated them. We put George in a bedroom and left Butch in the dining room. The experiment lasted less than half a day. We just couldn't stand their earsplitting shrieks as they called to each other.

There is nothing like a myna bird to make you more careful of your speech. When Butch says, "Stanley, aren't you finished yet?" in just my exasperated, impatient tone of voice, I resolve to be more patient. When my husband hears Butch mumbling, "This is Dr. Norman," he knows how he answers the telephone when he's tired and sleepy. When we kneel for worship and hear Butch begin in a reverent tone of voice, "Our kind heavenly Father," we learn about ourselves, too. And the children, profiting from Raymond's experience, are extremely careful what they say when Butch is around.

I could have gotten many things with my income tax refund that year. Clothes—but they would be out of style by now. I could have gotten books, but likely I would have read and forgotten them after all this time. Instead, I got Butch, who will never be out of style or forgotten. He is a clown, a tattletale, a bundle of black impudence, and a joy forever.

Pretty Girl

Louise came to collect our insurance premiums every month, and when one day I found her at the door just a week after she'd made her usual visit, I must have looked as puzzled as I felt.

"No, my dear," she said with a smile, "I've not come to collect again so soon. I have a problem I hope you can help me with."

"I'm willing to try," I offered.

"I've noticed you like animals," she began, "and always have several around. Could you—or would you—take one more?"

"It depends on the animal," I said.

"It's a dog, a perfectly beautiful dog. We found her almost frozen outside our office building and brought her inside. There we fed her and kept her all day. But when work ended for the day, somebody had to take her home. Everybody else had some reason why he couldn't, so I ended up with her. I've had her a week, but I can't keep her any longer." Then, either by accident or by design, she brought out the one argument I could not resist. "If you can't take her," she said, "I'll have to give her to the Humane Society!"

"I have room for one more dog," I said. "Usually we have two, but right now we have only one. When do you want to bring her out?"

"I'll go home and get her right now," Louise said, and smiled again.

After she left, I thought of all the questions I should have asked but didn't. How big was the dog? How old? What kind? Was she gentle? Oh, well, I'd already accepted her, and if she didn't fit in with the family, I'd soon be doing what Louise had been doing—trying to find a home for the animal.

Within the hour Louise returned with the dog.

"What's her name?" I asked first.

"My husband calls her Dagmar," Louise replied, "but we've had her such a short time that I doubt it means anything to her. You probably could name her whatever you like."

"I don't think she looks like the Dagmar type," I commented.

The dog was medium-sized and had rather long black

hair with a glossy sheen to it. Her plumed tail waved slowly to and fro as she looked from one of us to the other.

"Come here, pretty girl," I said, and she came at once.

The dog began to pant in the warm house. Her tongue contained a few dark blue-gray splotches.

"She must be part chow," I remarked.

"Yes, she is," Louise said. "I took her to a veterinarian, and he says she is half chow and half cocker. He says that is a good mixture. She's about two years old, he thinks. He can't guarantee what condition she's in, though."

"She looks fine," I observed. "Look how glossy her fur is. That's a good sign of health."

"Well, she'd been outside for some time, and we can't tell what her condition really is," Louise repeated.

"We'll take good care of her, and she'll be fine," I promised.

Louise smiled faintly and shook her head slightly as if we had had a cross-up in communication somewhere along the line. Then she went home.

The lovely black dog made herself right at home with us. From the first time I spoke to her we never called her anything but Pretty Girl. She wasn't the type to romp and play with the children, preferring to spend her time with me in the house.

One of our pets then was a white rabbit that had the run of the house. He was a good-sized rabbit, but no match for a dog, and what dog won't chase a rabbit if he has a chance? The first time the rabbit hopped into the room with Pretty Girl, her ears pricked up and she sniffed eagerly.

"No, Pretty Girl!" I said firmly, putting my hand on her neck. She quieted and lay down at my feet.

Soon the rabbit hopped closer. The dog trembled, but didn't get up.

"No, Pretty Girl!" I repeated.

She looked at me and licked her chops, but that was all.

Then the rabbit hopped right between her front paws. Quickly I dropped my hand back on her neck, and for the third time I admonished, "No! No, Pretty Girl."

The rabbit stretched his head forward cautiously and touched his nose to hers. She turned her head to one side. From that moment I knew I could trust her not to hurt the rabbit. Even when he snuggled down between her paws for a nap, or jumped over her back, or rubbed his head along her side, she never showed any interest in him as prey. I'd said, "No!" and that was that.

Before we'd had her long, it became apparent that Pretty Girl was going to have pups. I commented on the fact to Louise the next time she came.

"Yes," she agreed. "Remember, I told you she might."

"You did?" I said, puzzled. I couldn't remember her mentioning any such thing.

"I told you we couldn't tell for sure what condition she was in," she reminded me.

"Oh!" I said. Now I knew what she'd meant by "condition." Strained through so many layers of needless delicacy, no wonder it hadn't been clear to me. I was accustomed to plainer talk.

Not too long after that a bit of commotion in the big closet at the head of the stairs woke me up. Half the size of an ordinary room, the closet had a window overlooking the roof of the back sun porch. The children used it for a playroom sometimes, and their voices had now awakened me.

"I think that's all," said one. "Let's change the sheet."

"All right," replied another. "I'll go get one."

"She's probably thirsty," interjected a third. "Better get her some water."

"And some bread and milk, too," suggested the first voice I'd heard.

I went to the bedroom door and saw two of the children coming down the stairs, evidently after a clean sheet, some water, and bread and milk.

"What are you up to at five thirty in the morning?" I asked.

"We've been helping Pretty Girl have her pups," Gigi explained. "I think she's through now, and we're going to give her some food and water and change her sheet."

"Get an old sheet from the ragbag," I ordered. "How many pups are there?"

"Seven, Mamma. And they're the cutest little things you ever saw!"

I went upstairs to see. Pretty Girl looked exhausted, but proud. Yes, I had to admit that the pups were just about the cutest I'd ever seen.

In a few days we moved Pretty Girl and her pups into the greenhouse. We feared that in the house the pups would start waddling around and tumble down the stairs. They weren't at all lonely in the greenhouse, for the children visited them as often as time permitted.

When the pups got their eyes open, they looked cuter than ever, but one in particular always captured our interest. A red-gold color, he had a white chest and a white ring around his neck. He looked as if someone had tied a white fur bib on him, so we named him "Bib." We thought his father must have been a collie.

My husband said that of course we couldn't keep any of the pups, not even a single one of them. From time to time he'd send out to the house someone he'd met that wanted a dog. Though Bib was by far the prettiest of the pups, whenever people looked interested in him, the children always managed to convince them that one of the other ones would be far more suitable for them. Finally, only Bib remained. And without anything ever being said about it directly, Bib stayed.

We put Bib and Pretty Girl outside to live as soon as Bib was old enough. They played endless games of tag on the lawn, chased the neighborhood cats, and when they grew tired, took naps under the front porch.

Passing through a big-footed, gangling adolescence, Bib grew into a compact, sturdy dog, showing more and more of his chow ancestry the older he grew. Though gentle with the family, he had an air about him that hinted he'd brook no nonsense from strangers.

Later it grew evident that Pretty Girl was going to have pups again. She had five, all black, and we felt sure the father was the big black Labrador from a couple of blocks down the street. For some reason the children showed no interest in keeping any of the pups, but because the pups were part Labrador, we had no trouble giving them away. In fact, we didn't have enough to go around to everybody who wanted one.

We moved to the country the following spring, and not long after that Pretty Girl had her third litter of pups. The night they were born a club meeting convened at our house. One of my friends insists that I met her at the door and told her that the children were riding the dog in the pasture and the horse was having pups in the barn. I do not remember making such a statement, but I do remember the children interrupting the meeting by running in to whisper to me that Pretty Girl had another pup, until finally all seven were born.

Again we had pups to give away. Daddy announced to the children that they *absolutely* could not keep a one of the pups. But somehow, the puppy the children liked best didn't find a home, and so "Chief," as they named him, joined Pretty Girl and Bib as the family dogs.

Then daddy made a decision. Since the children had managed to keep a pup out of all but one of Pretty Girl's litters, the only thing to do was to have the veterinarian perform surgery on Pretty Girl so she'd not have any more pups. Otherwise, at the rate we were going we'd soon have so many dogs at our house we wouldn't have any room for people.

So the next time he had a day off, my husband took Pretty Girl to the animal hospital. She would have her surgery the next day.

In midmorning the veterinarian called. "I have bad news, Mrs. Norman," he said. "Your dog died from the anesthetic before we ever got started on the surgery. I don't know what happened. Could we have your permission for an autopsy?"

"Yes, of course," I responded automatically.

Pretty Girl was gone. I'd have to tell the children when they came in from school, something I wasn't looking forward to.

Before noon the doctor called again. "We found the trouble," he said. "Your dog had hepatitis. She was just in the early stages. Had she been sick lately?"

"No," I replied. "The only thing I noticed different was that for the past two days she kept wanting to come in and stay in the house under the table all the time. That was unusual for her."

"Probably within forty-eight hours or so she would have gotten sick enough for you to recognize it," he commented.

"Could you have done anything for the hepatitis?" I asked.

"Yes, by catching it early. If you have any other dogs, you had better vaccinate them against it, though."

"I'll bring them right down," I said.

"If you'd like, I'll take care of the black dog's body for you so that you won't have to take it back home."

"I'd appreciate that very much." I sighed.

"I'm awful sorry it happened this way," he said. "It was just one of those things we can't foresee."

Bib and Chief now took over guarding our property. They were so gentle with us and with anyone else when we were around that we often joked that if a burglar ever attempted to enter our house, the dogs would help him. And then a burglar did try.

We went away one weekend. When we got home, we discovered signs that someone had tried to break into the house. Marks on the door showed where he had chipped the wood, but he had not entered the house. He'd had better luck with the garage, breaking and opening the sliding overhead door. But he had taken nothing. A small pool of dried blood just inside the door led us to believe that one of the dogs had taken a bite out of the burglar and kept him at bay there for a few minutes before he could escape.

The two dogs liked to run about the fields during the day, but when evening came, Bib stayed by the house while Chief would still wander. When a rabbit ventured into the yard at dusk, both dogs would give chase, but Bib would stop at our fence, and Chief would continue chasing the rabbit until he either caught it or it outdistanced him.

One night Chief decided to follow my brother when he walked the two miles into town. Less than half a mile from home he ran across the road in front of a car, which killed him instantly. The woman driving the car telephoned me in tears, offering to get us another dog or do anything she could to make up for it. I knew Chief's habit of dashing out into the road and assured her that I knew the accident wasn't her fault. I also told her we had all the dogs we needed and not to try to get us another one.

The next evening at dark Bib trotted out of the yard and down the road toward town. Was he remembering that Chief had gone down the road the night before and hadn't come home yet? Was he looking for his playmate? Every evening since then Bib starts off at dark and doesn't come home for several hours. He always goes off down the road toward town. Many times we see him along the road or on the streets of our little suburb as we drive around at night. He always returns home by bedtime, ready for guard duty.

Whenever I come home from an errand, Bib meets me at the car and, taking my hand in his mouth, walks me to the door. If I am carrying something and have my hands full, he takes the hem of my skirt and walks with me. He also escorts in the same manner certain friends of mine who visit me frequently, though he always takes hold of their skirts, never their hands, seeming to know that if he took the latter he might frighten them.

Bib always welcomes the men who deliver the milk and bread, read the electric meter, and fill the propane tanks, even if he's never met them before and even if no member of the family is home. We feel sure Bib can distinguish those who have legitimate reason to be on our property from those who have no business there. So far, he has never let us down.

André

It took a long time for poodles to make an impression on me, but when they did, it was a lasting one. In vain my friends showed off their poodles, extolling their virtues and trying in every way to coax me into joining their fan club. My lack of interest was so complete that I didn't even exert myself to resist, for resistance at least implies a bit of temptation. When I finally did succumb to the attractions of the poodle, it was so final and irrevocable that it astounded everyone. Perhaps the explanation lies in the fact that only after I became really well acquainted with a few poodles as individuals did I begin to love them as a family.

It all began with André. Madge, a nurse employed by my husband, introduced us. "I want you to come and meet André," she said as I walked into the clinic one afternoon. I followed her back to the nurses' station, not knowing whether André was a French diplomat, a professional charmer, or Madge's latest boyfriend. He turned out to be a bit of all three.

She had received André only two days before. His owner, a member of the USAF, awaited transfer overseas and felt that he couldn't take André with him. A mutual friend had suggested that Madge might like to have him, and so now, on her day off, she had brought him to the clinic for everybody to see.

Even as uninterested in poodles as I was, I could appreciate André's beauty and intelligence. His thick jet-black coat was clipped in what Madge said was a "Dutch cut." The word *elegant* came immediately to my mind—elegant without being in the least bit feminine. He shook hands with me as if he were sincerely glad to make my acquaintance. Madge had him perform his repertoire of tricks and informed me that he was so nearly human that he came to the bathroom to have his teeth brushed every morning and expected a nightcap of half a bottle of soft drink every evening at bedtime.

I saw André frequently after that first meeting. Each time he would jump up and put both front feet on my arm, then offer his paw for a handshake, all to express his pleasure at our meeting once again.

Madge loved to talk about her dog, so I learned a lot about André and poodles in general. André, she said, was a large miniature, lacking only a fraction of an inch of being in the standard class. While not registered with the American Kennel Club, he was eligible, and she planned to have him registered as soon as she could get around to it.

Her conversation often centered around André and his cute tricks and personality. Her affection for him was unmistakable. But to my shock, one day she told me she was going to give him away. And to my delight she said I could have him if I wanted him. Did I want him? I certainly did. But I wondered why she was giving him up.

She explained that as she was gone all day working, she thought he wasn't getting all the attention and companionship he should have. And recently he had taken to slipping outside whenever the door opened and not coming back until he felt good and ready, no matter how often she called him. Madge feared that on one of his rambles he'd get stolen or hit by a car, for she lived on a busy street. She would feel better, she said, if he belonged to our family, where people would surround him most of the day. Since we lived on an acreage outside the city, he could roam to his heart's content without the dangers that threatened him in town. And if we had him, she could come and see him whenever she had the chance.

So André came to live with us and be our dog. As with a human being who seems perfect as long as he is only an acquaintance and then shows all manner of trifling faults and idiosyncracies when he becomes a member of the family, so it was with André. And so, perhaps, he felt the same about me, for first of all I abolished the ritual of the soft-drink treat at bedtime. I reasoned that if such drinks were not good for children, they probably weren't suitable for André, either. Eventually he forgave me for that, even though I'm sure he never knew the reason for the measure I took.

45

I found that André was not always the perfect gentleman he'd seemed before. His makeup had hints of the spoiled child and swashbuckling bully, too. Perhaps, like anyone in a new situation, he was only trying to find out how far he could go and what we would allow him to do. It took some firm, no-nonsense handling to teach André that I simply would not tolerate his growling at me whenever I displeased him; that my husband, as head of the household and a busy physician, had the right to go and come as he pleased, no matter how ridiculous the hours seemed to André; and that the rest of the family and pets had a right to some of my attention also. After André fully understood such things, we once again established the balance of power in the household.

André thoroughly enjoyed the country, for now he had freedom to run as he never had before. He became familiar with all the other animals in the area. Sometimes I'd see him, hardly more than a black speck, running through the fields with a neighbor's dog. Once in a while he would come home so tired that he could hardly walk, and at least once he returned bearing eloquent testimony to the fact that somewhere along the way he'd met a skunk and had come out only second best. He was an indefatigable rabbit chaser, although to my knowledge he never did catch one. Still, he probably helped keep the darling pests out of my garden.

When the doorbell rang one fall day, I had no idea of the changes about to occur in my life and André's. When I opened the door, there stood a young friend of mine, Jerry Lake. I had first met him when he was a sophomore in academy. Now he was a junior in college. His parents had recently moved to an acreage a few miles from where we lived, and though Jerry and I met and talked often at the college, on the street, after church, and at junior camp, where I served as nurse and he as a counselor, it was the first time he had visited our home.

I had no sense of history repeating itself when I said to Jerry a little later, "I want you to meet André!"

André was at his best that day. Freshly clipped, confident, and self-assured, he exuded charm from the tip of his aristocratic muzzle to the fluffy pompon at the end of his short tail. He offered his paw to Jerry for a handshake, and his expression said plainly, "I'm so glad to meet you. I hope we'll be friends." It enchanted Jerry. If ever a young man fell in love with a dog at first sight, Jerry did.

Jerry visited us often after that, and from his talk I could tell he was spending some time reading and learning about poodles—a real concession for a busy premed student to make. On one visit he asked if I'd let André spend the night with him. I thought it would be all right. Later he stayed a weekend, and still later a whole week at Jerry's house.

One day he asked me if André had ever won any prizes. I answered rather proudly that as a puppy he had won second place in city-wide obedience trials, or so Madge had told me. Jerry seemed quite interested—he'd read more about obedience trials than I had. André was having his shampoo and clip that day, and when it was time to call for him, Jerry went along. He had many questions to ask the woman at the kennel. Impressed by his intelligent interest, she lent him some material on poodle training.

The next day Jerry was back. Would I mind if he gave André a refresher course in obedience, he asked. Of course I didn't mind. Then he said rather hesitantly, "I'd probably have to keep him over at home for at least three weeks."

"That will be all right," I replied, "as long as you bring him back to spend the night with us at least once a week."

Jerry agreed, snapped André's leash on, and they left. None of the three of us realized it then, but that moment marked the beginning of André's transfer of ownership.

Faithful to his promise, Jerry brought André back to stay at least one night a week at home with us during the three weeks. They both delighted in showing the progress they'd made in the obedience exercises. Up to then André had just been relearning the exercises he'd done as a puppy. Now Jerry wanted to teach him new tricks, necessitating his keeping André at his own home more and more. As his pre-med classes and labs took more of Jerry's time, our visits with André grew less and less frequent. Eventually I couldn't even remember anymore when he'd spent his last weekend at home. Finally my husband and I decided to give André to Jerry for his own.

It hadn't been hard to see where André's heart lay. We had only to watch how willingly—how gladly—André jumped into Jerry's car when it was time to go. Oh, when he saw us, André always wiggled with joy so hard that we feared he'd break in two, but when the visits ended, André knew where home was, and that was with Jerry.

It astounded Jerry when I told him we'd decided to let him have the poodle. "I can't take André," he protested. "He's your dog!"

"Not really," I said. "He's yours."

Jerry grinned sheepishly. "I know I've been keeping him an awful lot and all that, but I never think of him as belonging to me."

"Well, he belongs to you now," I insisted. "We know he'll be happier with you."

Finally Jerry gave in, and André had a new master.

The following summer the college chose Jerry to go as a student missionary to Peru, and of course André had to remain behind. So did Lori, Jerry's fiancée. They had to postpone their June wedding date to August.

André, too, seemed lonely, so Jerry's mother often took him with her in the car. One day as they drove along, André became greatly excited, whimpering, scrabbling at the windows, and wagging his short tail nearly off. Mrs. Lake was puzzled, unable to account for his behavior, until she noticed that they were almost even with our mailbox. Turning up the drive, she brought André in for a visit. He was overjoyed to see us, and after making an appropriate fuss over each one of us individually, he made a tour of the whole property—garage, barn, pasture, and creek—and renewed his acquaintance with all the other animals on the place. Then he was ready to go home and resume his wait for Jerry.

The summer eventually ended—to Lori and André it must have seemed interminable. But at last Jerry arrived home, and the wedding took place as planned. André had the same master, but a new family that now included Lori.

I have no doubt that in Jerry the poodle found one to whom he could give his wholehearted devotion. Oh, yes, he loved the rest of us, but until Jerry came along, I have the feeling André was just marking time.

Fuffy

If André began my surrender to the famous poodle charm, a little black imp named Fuffy made it complete and unconditional.

I first met Fuffy when I took André to get clipped one day. She came dancing and prancing, to give me such a welcome as would swell any ego to outsize proportions. Naturally, I thought her adorable. Even without the flattering fuss she made over me, I would have thought so. She was a bouncing, button-nosed, black-eyed, four-legged ball of nylon yarn. It was love at first sight, but when her owner offered her to me at about half the going rate for poodles, I hesitated. After all, I had a houseful of animals, and I knew my husband's reaction to another would be negative. But I did promise to think it over until I came back for André that afternoon.

All day long I thought about it. Finally I came to the reluctant conclusion that, though I was mightily attracted to that puppy, I'd better forgo the pleasure of being her owner. As soon as I walked into the kennel, she changed my mind as easily as if she got her daily exercise by reversing decisions. She acted as if she'd spent the whole miserable day just moping about, waiting for my return. Jumping up on her hind legs, she begged with pleading little squeals for me to hold her. When I picked her up, her wet little tongue licked me breathless and her front feet beat a fast tattoo on my shoulder. What else could I do but get out my checkbook and pay for her?

Possibly in anticipation of my reacting just the way I did, the woman at the kennel had given the puppy a shampoo and puppy clip; and as I ran my hands over her soft coat, I found a name for her—Nylon Velvet. We'd call her Velvet for short.

André, of course, came out looking extremely smart in his Dutch cut and evinced no surprise whatever when I put both him and Velvet into the car for the ride home. Perhaps she had somehow communicated her plan to him during the preceding hours.

The children were thrilled with her, and she with them. Then late in the day I took her up to the clinic to introduce her to my husband. He had remained there alone doing some of his bookwork. Although she showed plainly that she thought he was wonderful, the niggling little suspicion I'd had that she accorded everyone the same enthusiastic affection she'd given me proved to be unfounded. She left no doubt about whose dog she was—mine! Still, her attitude disarmed him to the point that his reaction to another pet was surprisingly favorable. My argument that we could sell her pups, whenever she had any, for nice sums, he found interesting but unnecessary. Velvet made it on the strength of her own personality.

After winning my husband's approval, she proceeded to thoroughly investigate the clinic. She had dozens of new things to smell and savor and file away in a retentive brain. Even human beings, with their dull olfactory organs, realize that hospitals and doctors' offices have quite distinctive odors, and to a dog's keen sense of smell, it must have been a veritable kaleidoscope. From that evening on she loved to visit the clinic, where she was a favorite with all the employees.

Shortly after we got her, Velvet had a siege of bronchitis, which made it necessary to take her to the veterinarian. A few injections of antibiotics helped her over the acute stage, but her cough lingered for weeks. I began to wonder if she would ever be strong and healthy, but the cough grew less frequent and milder, and finally disappeared altogether.

The name Velvet was not quite right for her, I began to think. Velvet, though soft and pliable, is a rather formal fabric, and the puppy certainly did not fit that image. Besides, the name wasn't enough of a diminutive to suit me. Soon I found myself calling her Fuffet, remembering how my baby sister had admired a velvet dress I'd had as a teenager, running her chubby hands over its soft folds and saying, "I just wuv your pwitty fuffet dwess." And Fuffet turned into Fuffy, which became her permanent name, except on her registration papers, where she bore the dignified title of "Nylon Velvet."

Fuffy was a house dog. After a run in the morning she seemed content to stay inside most of the day unless I went outside. Always affectionate, she really outdid herself when I returned after a morning's absence. Her obvious delight at my return could always soothe my battered ego after a difficult class period.

Though she was sweet and loving, I had the feeling that as poodles went, Fuffy was the beautiful but dumb type. The kennel had her "paper-trained" when we got her, and she never advanced any further. Perhaps I am better at teaching people than poodles, because in spite of all my efforts, she remained "paper-trained," and no more. Even though I took her outside several times a day, I still had to leave papers strategically placed around the house to prevent disaster betweentimes.

It was a great day for all of us when Fuffy graduated from her puppy trim to a Dutch cut to match André's. She looked so grown-up and acted as proud and vain as a girl in her first formal. During the same trip to the kennel I met Fuffy's sister, Banner. Banner was a retiring, shy poodle, but extremely beautiful. Instead of being jet black like Fuffy, Banner had lovely chocolate brown fur. The kennel was grooming her as a show dog. The owner of the kennel told me that Fuffy, too, had the makings of a good show dog, with an excellent chance to win her championship. She explained that poodles are incorrigible hams and thoroughly enjoy being exhibited in the shows—and I knew that if that were true of most poodles, it would be doubly so of vain little Fuffy. However, when I learned from further questioning that it took well over a year to develop a good show coat, and it required at least an hour of grooming a day, I decided

Fuffy would have to remain ignorant of the joys of show doghood. After all, I could hardly spare an hour a day for my own grooming, so that much time for Fuffy was out of the question.

The kennel owner remarked to me several times that Fuffy was the friendliest, best-natured dog she'd ever seen. And for that I've been extremely grateful, for her loving disposition did much to ease the way when we added two new members to our family.

Don and Stan were fourteen and twelve, respectively, when they came to live with us. We had been asked to give them foster-home care, and we accepted, on the condition that we'd be allowed to adopt them later. We received permission, and so I drove the 120 miles to get them. Conversation was halting and difficult on the ride back. I had met Stanley only briefly three years earlier, and had never met Don before, so naturally the two brothers were somewhat fearful and uneasy as to what lay before them. How would the other four children accept them? I had no fears on that point, but Don and Stanley had no way of knowing how they would be welcomed. That, and a thousand other questions, must have tormented them during the ride home.

As soon as the car stopped in the driveway, Fuffy came flying out to give us her usual exuberant welcome. Stan picked her up and held her close, and several hours later he exclaimed, "I knew I wanted to stay as soon as I saw that little black dog."

For over a week Stan held Fuffy nearly every waking moment. We soon learned to gauge his emotional barometer by the amount of time he held her. I saw how soothing her love could be to a bruised heart, and I blessed her for her healing gift. As time went by, and he became more secure and certain of his place in our affections, he depended less and less on Fuffy for love, but when he needed her, she was there.

When the time neared for Fuffy to have her first litter of pups, I made careful plans. I had watched her diet closely, had been more faithful in giving her vitamins and minerals than I was in taking them myself, and had read all I could on the subject of making her approaching motherhood as easy as possible.

Friends had told me that likely one out of four of Fuffy's puppies would be brown like Banner, for she had many brown poodles in her ancestry. I planned to name the brown one Brown Velvet or Brown Corduroy and go to almost any lengths to get my husband to let me keep it.

Five days before the puppies' expected arrival, I called the kennel and made an appointment for her to get a puppy cut the next day. Then I went into town to see if I could find a large cardboard box to use as a delivery room. The poodle book had said to get some burlap to tack on the floor of the box to provide traction for the puppies' feet, so I also had that on the shopping list.

The burlap proved difficult to find. When I returned home that evening much later than I had expected, the children met me with the news that Fuffy had delivered her "pups" already—only *one,* and it was stillborn. It was a bitter disappointment. Fuffy was playing around as if nothing in the world had taken place, but when I sat down, she jumped up on the couch beside me and placed her head in my lap.

Gigi told me she had examined the puppy immediately after its birth and knew he was dead, so she had had the boys bury it. He had been black, she said. Gigi wanted to be a doctor, and I knew that if her instincts and healing touch were as sure with people as they were with animals, she would be an outstanding physician.

As we sat there talking of our disappointment, Fuffy suddenly sat up and delivered a second puppy on the cushion beside me. And it was alive—a little black female, five days premature.

After delivering the puppy, empty-headed little Fuffy then abdicated the responsibilities of motherhood and completely ignored her child. She refused to let it nurse voluntarily, so we fed it with a doll bottle whenever we failed in holding Fuffy down long enough for it to get all it wanted. I thought of Isaiah 49:15, "Can a woman forget her sucking child, that she should not have compassion on the son of her womb? yea, they may forget, yet will I not forget thee." Fuffy did all she could to forget hers. She wouldn't cuddle it and keep it warm, so the electric heating pad substituted for her. Even so, we had to watch Fuffy, for if she did happen to think about her little one, she'd drag the little thing off the heating pad and shove it onto the cold floor in a dark corner under Gigi's bed. At night Gigi kept the puppy in bed with her so that it could keep warm. Each morning we got up with our hearts in our mouths, wondering whether it had survived the night. Sometimes, if the puppy happened to cry during the day, Fuffy would bring it into the living room and deposit it under my chair. Walking away without a backward glance, her whole attitude declared, "This was your idea in the first place. Now you take care of it!"

For two weeks we worked to teach Fuffy the proper behavior for a young mother. And at the end of that time, if she did not show all the devotion we felt she should, at least she cared for the puppy adequately. She let it nurse when it was hungry, and part of the time she lay down beside it on the heating pad, letting it snuggle next to her. Eventually her maternal instincts sharpened, and she became quite fond of her little daughter, whom we called Missy.

We had promised Missy to a friend of ours who had always wanted a dog. Because our friend had allergies, the doctors had advised her against having pets at all, but even people who have allergies can sometimes tolerate a poodle, because poodles don't shed hair. Between us we'd decided that she'd see how things worked out. If all went well, she'd keep Missy. But if her allergies got worse, we'd take the pup back.

In the meantime, we waited for Missy to grow old enough to leave her mother. Fuffy spent considerable time playing with Missy and, surprisingly enough, never seemed jealous of the attention we gave the little one. Missy still slept with Gigi at night, but she spent her daytime naps with a stuffed toy we had bought for her—a plush mouse nearly as big as herself. We called it Missy's sleepy-mouse. Again Fuffy surprised us. Although she and Missy chased the same balls, played tug-of-war with the same socks, and chewed the same rawhide bones, she left Missy's sleepy-mouse strictly alone.

Early one morning an odd sound coming from the living room awakened me. I didn't find out what it was that day, but the following morning I heard it again, and that time I managed to trace it to its source. Missy was trying to learn to growl, and I'd heard her practicing.

At last the day came when Missy and her sleepy-mouse went to their new home. We awaited the verdict rather anxiously, but all went well, and Missy, rechristened Priscilla, became a cherished pet. Smaller than Fuffy, with Fuffy's jet-black coat and loving ways, but with far greater intelligence, Priscilla is an outstanding poodle, bringing pleasure to her family and all who know her.

In spite of her initial neglect, Fuffy had grown to love her puppy and missed her for a while, but she was never one to brood long over anything. She still acted like a puppy herself, and I felt sure that she'd never grow up.

The following fall Fuffy gave birth to a litter of four puppies and attended them with a solicitude heartwarming to behold. To say that her display of motherhood surprised us is putting it mildly. The only disappointment I had was that the brown puppy I'd hoped for did not appear in the litter.

One puppy I watched with particular interest. She was the smallest of the litter, but the word *runt* surely did not apply to the little charmer. Already her muzzle was more slender than those of the others, she was more alert and intelligent, and her coat was heavy and curled so prettily around her face that we called her Ruffles.

One day after the puppies had their eyes open, I took them up to the owner of the kennel to get an expert's opinion of them. She examined each of them carefully. "They are all fine puppies," she said, "but this one," picking up Ruffles, "is one of the finest I've ever seen. Keep her, if you possibly can. She is going to be outstanding."

"I don't see how I can keep her, much as I'd like to," I said, pleased that I'd been smart enough to spot Ruffles as a winner from the beginning. "There's always the problem of too many animals at our house."

"Well, if I were you, I'd get rid of the mother if I had to, but I'd keep this pup," she advised.

Get rid of Fuffy? I should say not! But maybe I could convince my husband that we should keep such a prize dog as Ruffles anyway. It was a vain hope. I had always known that someday my long-suffering husband would put his foot down firmly and say, "Enough is enough," and to my sorrow it came this time. He did, however, come up with what he considered a compromise. We'd give Ruffles to his associate's wife, Carol, for Christmas—we'd already planned to give her one of the pups—and then we'd be able to see Ruffles now and then.

Ten days before Christmas we had the annual clinic Christmas party. We presented Ruffles, resplendent in a red ribbon bow, to Carol. Carol's daughter, Lisa, received a tiny kitten, and the two baby animals were the stars of the Christmas party.

Tragedy struck five days later. Carol had gone to school to pick up the children. On their return home they could find neither the puppy nor the kitty. Nearly an hour of frenzied searching and calling went by, and still the pets were missing. Finally, in a snatching-at-straws gesture, one of the children began looking in dresser drawers—and in one found the little animals crammed down among the clothes, as though someone had stuffed them in hastily and slammed the drawer shut. Both were barely alive when found. A frantic dash to the animal hospital saved the cat, but it was too late for Ruffles. She died within minutes after reaching the hospital.

We never knew who put them into that drawer. We supposed some neighborhood child did it, meaning it for a joke, but we never found out for sure.

The children cried themselves to sleep, and we hurried to bring them the puppy that most closely resembled Ruffles. They loved her, but I'm sure that in their hearts, as well as in mine, there was only one Ruffles.

We also gave the other two puppies away as Christmas gifts. Somehow we couldn't bring ourselves to sell them. As it is, they are with friends, and we can see them often. Besides that, we have taken practical steps toward spreading the joys of poodle ownership.

In late February my husband and I were spending a rare

evening out at the home of one of the couples to whom we'd given a pup. We had had a wonderful time, probably because my husband so seldom can find time to relax and visit. Now as we sat laughing and talking, he decided to call home and check on the children, even though it was not yet ten o'clock. As he talked, he began to sound quite distressed. I listened anxiously as he said, "What? . . . When did it happen? . . . Just now? . . . You're sure? . . . Well, we'll see!" Then turning to me, he said, "Honey, the children found Fuffy dead out by the driveway. A car hit her."

Our hostess spoke up immediately. "You may have back the puppy you gave us. It will help you to have one of Fuffy's pups." It was an offer straight from the heart, for she adored the little pup she called Dupie.

"Thank you, but no," I replied. "No dog can replace Fuffy, and taking Dupie would leave you unhappy without helping me, except as a reminder of your unselfishness. I do appreciate the offer, though. You can't possibly imagine how much."

My husband asked, "Do you want to go home?"

"Yes, I think I do," I replied. After hasty, subdued good-byes, we left.

My mind kept shying away from the picture of Fuffy's little black body leaping joyously out in the dark to welcome some visitor, only to have a lethal wheel hit her. My husband had said she died instantly.

The children had thoughtfully removed Fuffy's food and water dishes from the kitchen and her toys from the living room, so that I would not have to face those sad reminders when I came in. Then they had all gone quietly to bed. And as always, after I'd been out for an evening, I went to each child's room to check and see that all was well before going to bed. When I got to Gigi's room, I found her asleep. At the foot of her bed, placed on a folded white towel, lay Fuffy's body, as naturally as if she, too, were only asleep.

I missed Fuffy more than I'd dreamed possible. I missed her from her first little bark in the morning, her playfulness during the day, her love and companionship, to the last contented little sigh she always gave as she settled herself in front of my bedroom door at night.

Dear little Fuffy, dashing headlong at life and through life and finally beyond life. Her name will never be forgotten as long as Butch once in a while recalls to mind that long ago he used to call, "Fuffy! Come here, Fuffy!" and a vibrant little bundle of black energy would come to prance around his cage. And so he tries it again, to see if maybe once more she will respond to his call. "Fuffy, come here! Come on, now, Fuffy!"

Mick

The receptionist called me from the clinic. "Mrs. Norman, there is a Mrs. Harvey here, and she wants to know if you'd like a poodle."

Would I like a poodle? What a silly question! By now I liked all poodles, though since Fuffy's death some months before I'd not had one of my own.

Within seconds I had Mrs. Harvey on the phone, bombarding her with questions.

How big was the poodle? A large miniature. "Probably about André's size," I thought to myself.

What was his name? Mickie—Mick, for short.

What color? Black.

Then Mrs. Harvey explained why she couldn't keep him. To begin with, her brother had purchased Mick as a puppy. The man had mistreated him, so his wife had given the animal to Mrs. Harvey. It had been a struggle financially for Mrs. Harvey to pay for keeping him trimmed and to buy medicine for the arthritis he suffered from, but somehow she had managed. Now, however, she was going to move into an apartment which did not allow pets, and she had to find a home for Mick. Since she had been my husband's patient for years, she had heard from him of my interest in animals and thought that just possibly I'd like to have Mick.

We made arrangements for her to bring the dog out the next day. The thought of having a poodle in the house again elated me. But I must say that my first glimpse of Mick left me considerably disappointed. Accustomed to the jet black of Fuffy's coat, it never occurred to me that a poodle labeled "black" would look any other way. Mick was a dull, dirty black, with one white foot and a white patch on his chest, and his moustache was brown—it actually looked tobacco stained. If I had not already said I'd take him, I would have refused to accept him. And yet it was plain that the Harveys hated to give him up, so he must have been a lovable dog.

Before she left, Mrs. Harvey showed us all the tricks Mick could do. He "spoke" for a cookie, sat and stood up, shook hands, rolled over and played "dead dog" with one paw over his eyes. Then she placed a cookie in front of him and said, "No, Mick!" While the rest of us urged him to eat it, he steadfastly refused until she told him it was all right— then it disappeared instantly.

After I told her that she was welcome to visit him at any time, she left Mick and me to become acquainted. The dog seemed to understand the change, and I suppose I should be ashamed to admit that he accepted me sooner than I did him, although it is true. He was shaggy, much in need of a trim. So I made an appointment for it to be done several days later. When I went to get him, he came strutting out as if to ask, "Well, do you like me any better now that I look like a proper poodle?" I did. I admit it.

When I knew Mick better, I found much to appreciate. Whereas André had been suave and debonair, Mick had an air of rough camaraderie. In his smart Dutch clip he reminded me of a lumberjack in a tuxedo, the white patch on his chest helping the illusion.

I found it hard not to compare Mick with André, since both were large miniatures, large males, and about the same age. As I grew more familiar with Mick, I found the comparisons more and more in his favor. In the matter of beauty and elegance, André had Mick beat a mile, but in overall adjustment Mick was by far the winner. André was sensitive to his own feelings; Mick, to those of others. André had confidence in his own looks and charm; Mick had confidence in his own worth. Of course I may have been reading human traits into the two poodles, but that is how it seemed to me.

Mick, as André before him, had to receive acceptance by Bib, but after the initial noisy set-to, the lifting of lips and snarls, they came to an agreement as to each one's place in the scheme of things, and mostly all went well.

During the first summer Mick lived with us, we went on several three-day camping trips. Each time we left the poodle to board at the kennel. When it came time for our two-week vacation, we hated to deposit him at the kennel for such a length of time, but we knew of no one else with whom to leave him. Three days before we planned to go, Mrs. Harvey came to see him. When she learned of our problem, she offered at once to take him for a visit; she felt sure the landlord wouldn't mind for only two weeks.

On our return, she brought him back early in the morning and told us how unhappy he'd been. He had seemed glad to see them all again, but detested being shut up in the apartment or tied to a chain outside.

When we finally released him at home again, he ran in circles all over the fields back of the house, and finally disappeared. At noon we called him for dinner, but he didn't come. At last, about six in the evening, he came up the driveway, his tongue hanging out, so exhausted he could barely put one foot ahead of the other. But he knew he was home. He had evidently examined all his familiar haunts for miles around, and, finding everything satisfactory, he now could rest.

The next summer when vacation time came, we decided it would be better for all the pets to remain at home in their familiar surroundings and have someone come in two or three times a day and take care of them. The first day we were gone the girl in charge of the animals arrived late, and found that Mick, in his utter dismay at being left at home, had gone into my bedroom closet and pulled three dresses off their hangers and ripped them to pieces. Then he had done the same to the bedspread and top sheet on the bed.

I had heard stories of poodles destroying their owner's property when angry, but I had never had it happen to us before. When I arrived home and someone asked me if I planned to punish Mick, I decided against it. After a lapse of three weeks, how could he know why I was chastising him? When I reflected on the time Mick had been with us, I realized I'd never so much as had to scold him for anything.

That, I thought, was quite a good record. And even though his breach of behavior had been a drastic one, anyone is entitled to one mistake.

One of Mick's most endearing traits was his feeling for the small and helpless. It showed in his championship of Casey, a small Keeshond puppy we acquired.

The children and I saw Casey and several of his brothers and sisters at Mary's Pet Store. They had fine furry coats, a dense gray tipped with silver. Their oversized ears pricked up, and their little pointed, foxlike faces grinned impudently at us. Mary told us that Keeshonds were related to huskies and were wonderful watchdogs. They originated in Holland, where people used them to guard barges on the canals.

Naturally we wanted one of the fascinating dogs, but we knew daddy's rule—no more dogs. Still, the next time the family went for a drive, someone directed daddy down the street on which the pet store was located; someone else mentioned that we were getting low on myna bird food; and before long all of us, daddy included, stood watching the Keeshond puppies in their display pen. And even though he said he was onto us all along, it was he who chose and paid for the pup we brought home. He justified his purchase by saying that Casey would be a good companion for Bib, now that Chief was dead, and later he'd be a valuable watchdog.

Bib, however, wasn't interested in any such plans. Usually the gentlest of dogs, he was definitely snappish toward Casey. One day Casey ran up and pawed at Bib, trying to entice him into a game. Bib, with weightier matters on his mind, snarled and snapped at the younger dog. Mick had observed the whole thing. With indignation explicit in every line of his body, he marched over to Bib and uttered several threatening growls. I could imagine him saying, "Leave the little fellow alone, or I'll tear you apart!" And to my amusement Bib looked far more abashed than he ever did at one of my scoldings.

Mick then went over, licked Casey consolingly behind the ear, and the two of them ran off for the romp Casey had been begging for from Bib. The little episode caused us to nickname Mick "Big Brother" part of the time. Whenever Casey, as the youngest and newest of our pets, frequently got the worst of a bout with Skee or "THAT COATI!" and let his howls ascend to the heavens, someone would say, "Run on to Big Brother, now. He'll take care of you." And Mick did, too.

Sometimes, though, when the tables turned and Casey too roughly treated "THAT COATI!" or Skee, Mick taught him in no uncertain terms that his protection was not to become a license for bullying and that the others in the family were entitled to their share of consideration.

As mentioned earlier, Mick suffered from arthritis. Mrs. Harvey had given us a large bottle of medicine for him and told us Mick was good about taking it. During his second winter with us he had several periods of lameness. We had to dose him with the white pills three or four times a day. He swallowed them without trouble, and they always helped.

Because of his arthritis and the cold that winter, we did not have Mick trimmed as usual, but let his coat grow long and shaggy, only cutting it away from his eyes. By spring he looked twice his size because of his heavy coat. At last, when the weather grew warm and settled, Mick got his clip. He looked neat and "proper-poodle," and he knew it, too.

On the way home from the kennel I remarked to Stanley, "I wonder what Casey will think of Mick's new haircut. Mick's been shaggy ever since we got Casey." And even though I wondered casually about it at that moment, I was totally unprepared for Casey's reaction to the "new" Mick.

When we drove into the driveway, the children came out to welcome Mick home, and for the next several minutes Mick went from one to the other to be petted and admired, reveling in the attention.

I happened to glance over at Casey standing beside the garage and saw his ears pricked up so high it looked as if any moment they might fly off his head, and on his foxlike face an expression of utter astonishment. At the same moment Stanley picked him up and said kindly, "Come on over and see Mick, Casey."

If the strange new creature was Mick, Casey didn't realize it. Scrabbling frantically, he managed to get away from Stanley and dashed away, ki-yiing in terror. Stanley ran and caught him. Bringing him back, he endeavored to explain. "It's only Mick, Casey," Stanley pleaded. "You know Mick."

Casey's actions replied, "I know Mick, but I don't know who that is. I'm not even sure *what* it is!" And again he got loose and ran off howling with fright.

Mick, in the meantime, unaware of all the fuss, just trotted around the yard. The rest of us laughed ourselves weak.

When I could finally speak, I said, "Children, leave them alone. Let's just sit down here and see what happens."

We all sat on the stones bordering the drive. When Mick saw the rest of us taking it easy, he did, too, settling himself in the middle of the drive in front of the kitchen door.

Several minutes later Casey first peeked, then stepped hesitantly around the corner of the garage. Spying Mick, he stopped, his tail, usually curled over his back, tucked down as far as it would go. Then he advanced, one cautious step at a time—stiff-legged, poised for instant departure—whimpering, half in perplexity, half in fear. After he had taken several steps, Mick turned and glanced mildly in his direction. Casey exploded into flight, shrieking his alarm. The poodle gazed after him in bewilderment, plainly wondering what had gotten into his little friend. If Mick had gone after him to see what the trouble was, I fear Casey's heart might not have stood the strain.

The incident recurred several times, each time Casey coming a bit closer and holding his ground a fraction of a minute longer. At last he managed to walk completely around Mick from a distance of nine or ten feet away, so that he viewed him in fearful fascination from every angle. Several hours later he had grown bold enough to romp close to Mick, taking care to keep out of reach, still not sure the "duded-up" creature was Big Brother despite the familiar smell. It took at least four days before they reestablished their old comradeship.

I wondered later what gymnastics poor little Casey's mental processes must have performed during the episode. Did he fear that the strange animal had eaten Mick? Was his frame of reference momentarily destroyed by the being that smelled exactly like Mick but looked like nothing he'd ever seen before? Other strange dogs he'd seen and taken in stride, but something about this blend of the strange and familiar left him gibbering with anxiety.

Mick loved to ride in the car and always quivered with eagerness when he thought he had a chance to go with me. He would stick his head out the window, squint his eyes against the wind stream which whipped his ears back like tasseled wings, and look the picture of enjoyment.

One day he kept leaning farther and farther out the window until the inevitable happened. The law of gravity laid hold of him, and he pitched out, head over heels. Luckily, he landed in the weeds beside the road. When I looked back, after getting the car stopped, I saw him scrambling back onto the blacktop. He looked chagrined, as if I'd scolded.

I called to him. He hesitated, then turned and started in a slow trot toward home. I called again, and this time he turned and reluctantly came to me. He got in the car, but he sat right in the middle of the seat, an extremely subdued dog. It didn't last long—before we reached home, he had stuck his head out the window again. Since then he's never leaned out far enough to tempt a tumble.

Despite such interruptions, Mick continues his responsibilities around the property, informing Bib that his place is *not* in the house, tolerating Casey inside for a short time as a concession to his youth, deciding who is at fault in the melees between Skee and "THAT COATI!," chasing the aggressor away and comforting the victim, taking back talk from "THAT COATI!" when he's in a saucy mood, and, as time permits, supervising the surrounding countryside. He warns indiscriminately of friend and foe alike, to the near destruction of our eardrums. Each night he tries to sleep under our bed, evidently for protection, but whether his or ours, I've not been able to ascertain.

Whenever Mrs. Harvey comes to see him, he wags his tail, shakes hands with her, and lets her know he's glad she came. Next he comes to me, looks pleadingly into my face, and then disappears until she has gone. Except for that disappearing act, I'd never be able to interpret that pleading look that says, "Don't send me back. I like it here. I'm your dog."

Mick need not fear. As a part of the family his place is secure, for how could I handle the rest of the gang without the help of my lumberjack in his fancy tuxedo?

"THAT COATI!"

It's a pity to be absentminded, but to this day I don't remember ordering that animal. But when the pet shop called me and said my pet had arrived, I went out of curiosity—and lost my heart to a coatimundi. A tiny reddish-brown ball of fur, he clung to the bars halfway up the side of the cage, his long wiggling nose poked out through the wire; and he was twittering like a bird. I thought he was just about the cutest little bit of a thing I'd ever seen.

Mary, the pet shop owner, took him out of the cage and placed him on the counter. He immediately trotted over to a loaf of raisin bread, and before we could stop him, he had torn open the wrapper and grabbed a slice of bread, from which he dug the raisins and devoured them.

While Mary hunted up a box for me to take him home in, I got acquainted with my pet. He looked like a dog that a committee had put together. His head was shaped like an opossum's, although his nose was more elongated, almost like an anteater's; he walked like the bears in Yellowstone Park; his tail was fluffy and ringed like a raccoon's; and he was the color of a red squirrel. (Later we thought he'd gotten his claws from a badger.)

Mary told me what to feed him, and soon I arrived home with my newest pet. The encyclopedia I consulted told little, only that he came from the jungles of Mexico, Central America, or South America, would grow to be about two and one-half feet long and weigh about ten pounds, and that the Indians of Latin America often trained coatis as pets. He was, as I'd suspected, a member of the raccoon family.

Several days later, after he'd gotten used to living at our house, I took him to visit school. The children loved him, and he had a grand time—trotting along on the tables, sniffing at every pencil, book, and ruler. All the children had a chance to pet him and ask questions about him. When he got tired of their attention, he curled up in the crook of my arm and covered his eyes with his paws.

After a week I decided that his cage was too small for him, so I drew up plans and bought material for a new one, thinking it would provide a good Sunday-afternoon project for my three teen-aged sons. Somehow, though, baseball kept interfering, with the result that I built the cage myself. I felt tremendously proud of my accomplishment, though I knew I'd never be able to make my living as a carpenter.

The question of a name for the little fellow kept coming up, but somehow I couldn't decide on one, so we just kept calling him Coati.

One day, when we'd had him about six weeks, I noticed his feet were swollen. The next day they began to bleed. Wherever he went about the cage, little bloody footprints followed him. A few days later I saw that the end of his pretty fluffy tail was bare and scaly. Alarmed, I took him at once to see our family veterinarian.

"I think it must be some sort of allergy," the doctor said. "I'll give you some medicine and a special solution for his bath, and we'll see how he does." As he wrote out the directions for giving the medicine, he continued, "Sometimes these exotic pets never do adjust to our climate."

I looked at Coati, with his poor bleeding feet and great patches of his fur gone, and thought nothing in the world ever looked less exotic than he did at that moment.

I used the medicine faithfully, but somehow I felt we were approaching the whole thing from the wrong angle. His symptoms seemed to me to indicate more of a dietary deficiency than an allergy. He appeared to be better on the days he could go outside with the children for a while. They had discovered that he loved crickets, and they would turn over stones so that he could catch all the crickets he could stuff himself with. Once we gave him a tiny little garter snake to play with, and he devoured it with the same gusto. On the whole, I could see my pet was getting worse instead of better, so I asked Mary at the pet shop to write and ask for a diet for him. The answer came back—"strictly vegetarian."

When it came time for us to go on vacation, I left him with a friend. He was a pitiful sight. Even more of his fur had fallen off, his once-beautiful tail was bare and scaly, and his feet were still sore and bleeding. His appetite was good, but besides eating, all he wanted to do was snuggle down in my hands and sleep. Deciding I would depart from the strictly vegetarian diet and give him some dog food on the supposition that it would contain any vitamins he might be lacking, I left several cans with the friend who cared for him while we were gone.

One day during our vacation we stopped at a well-known reptile garden and zoo. There in a cage sat a full-grown coatimundi. A beautiful specimen, it had sleek, shiny fur and a fluffy tail. I immediately hunted up the keeper and asked him what he fed the animal.

"Monkey pellets," he replied.

I told him the problem I'd been having with my pet.

"I'll bet it's his diet," the man said. "Try giving him monkey pellets, and see if that doesn't help. And watch out when he gets well. He will be so full of mischief you'll hardly be able to put up with him."

I thanked him and promised to take his advice—if my coati was still alive when I got home. Secretly, I doubted that my gentle little creature would ever show a spark of mischief. He was different from other coatimundis—all he ever wanted to do was sleep.

Vacation over, I hurried to see about my pet. Yes, he was still alive, and I thought he seemed a little better. Happy to see us, he pressed the end of his funny little soft nose all over our faces and squeaked for joy.

I ordered the monkey pellets, and when they came, he loved them, dipping them, in true raccoon fashion, in his water dish before eating. In a short time his feet healed, then his fur began to grow back, and finally the day came when his ringed tail was as fluffy as it had been the day we got him. All that remained to remind us of his illness was his name. We'd grown so accustomed to saying, "Oh, you poor baby!" when he'd been sick and pathetic, that for a while afterward we just called him Baby—until he earned himself another name.

With his returning health he became extremely active. And he grew, though not as big as the encyclopedia had led us to believe he would. Further reading in a book entirely on animals informed us about many different kinds and sizes of coatis in South America. We decided he was one of the smaller kinds that live along the Amazon River.

He had always loved to curl up in my hands and sleep, with one hand completely covering him. My hand, however, couldn't keep pace with his new growth. One evening he seemed to realize that I was doing a poor job of covering him with my hand. He pulled it over his head, but that left his hindquarters uncovered, so he pushed the hand back, only to uncover his head. He tried to curl up in a little ball as he used to do, but that didn't work, either. Finally, huffing and squeaking indignantly, he got up and stalked away.

A book on coati care said that you must take a pet coati from his cage each day and play with him. When we first let ours out each day, he felt he had to investigate everything in the area. He'd climb up onto the table next to the bird cages, sending the two mynas and the canary into fluttering fits of anxiety. Next he would hunt up Mick, tease him into chasing him, and then from the safety of the back of the couch, dare the long-suffering poodle to come up and fight like a man. After that we had no way of telling what he'd do, and I found myself defending, excusing, apologizing, and pleading for my pet. It was during this period that he acquired what seems to be his permanent name—"THIS COATI!" or "THAT COATI!" as the case happens to be, complete with capitals and exclamation marks.

Perhaps it would be Raymond exclaiming, "Mother, 'THAT COATI!' came in and knocked my orchid plant over and broke off all the blooms!" And I could only reply, "Well, do you remember the time you put your pet duck in my greenhouse and he ate all the plants he could reach?"

Or maybe Gigi would complain, "Mother! 'THAT COATI!' climbed up onto my dresser and turned over my perfume and shampoo and everything!" And I promised to try to see that he didn't get in there again.

Or someone else would indignantly call, "Mother! How can I do my homework when 'THAT COATI!' keeps trying to turn the pages to see what's under them before I'm through reading them?"

Sometimes it's even my husband shouting, "Mother! Come and get 'THIS COATI!' off my neck. His claws are like needles, and I can't shave with him up here." That's when "THAT COATI!" goes back to his cage, and no "maybes" about it.

However, there isn't a member of the family who doesn't love "THAT COATI!" and each one insists "THAT COATI!" bites him more gently than he does everyone else. If sometimes they threaten to donate him to the zoo, other times they take turns making him ecstatically happy by scratching him with the battery-operated back scratcher daddy got for Christmas. And all agree that even though mother doesn't remember ordering "THAT COATI!" they are glad she did.

Little Jag and Skee

"I want a cheetah for my birthday," Ray announced at breakfast one morning in April. "I thought I'd tell you early so you'll have time to locate one before July."

"Absolutely not!" my husband said firmly. "I'm having no animals in this house that might tear my legs off when I come home from a house call in the middle of the night!"

"Well, then, an ocelot, maybe?" Ray inquired. His lack of disappointment over having the cheetah so quickly and definitely vetoed made me suspect he had had the ocelot in mind all along, and had only asked for the cheetah to make the ocelot sound gentler and more acceptable.

"No ocelot, either," replied my husband. "Some ocelots grow big as cheetahs, and you can't tell ahead of time which ones will get big and which ones will stay small." I wondered how he knew so much about them. Had he been anticipating such a request and mustered his arguments ahead of time?

"I want some kind of wildcat," Ray persisted. "There must be a small wildcat of some kind in the world that I could have for my birthday."

After breakfast I went to Mary's Pet Shop for information. Mary listened to my request, then suggested, "Why not get him a jaguarundi kitten? Jaguarundis grow to only about house-cat size, and they make good pets." I placed the order and went home, thinking what an addition a small yellow jungle cat with black spots would be to our household.

Time went by. Ray's birthday came, but the cat didn't. Forgetting about the cat, Ray wanted skin-diving equipment, or life wouldn't be worth living.

Since Ray had something else for his birthday, I reasoned I could claim the jaguarundi for myself. I decided to read up on the animal, and out came the encyclopedia. Away went my vision of a black-spotted yellow jungle kitty—the encyclopedia said that jaguarundis were either reddish-brown or black. For a moment I felt so disappointed that I thought of canceling the order; but my curiosity won out, and I decided to wait and see what it really looked like. Small head, said the encyclopedia, long body, short legs, long tail. In an animal book I found a picture of a jaguarundi all curled up in the corner of a cage, so I didn't learn a lot from that, except that jaguarundis don't look much like house cats.

During the first week in August Mary called to say the

kitten was ready for me to take home. She'd kept it for a week to be sure it was healthy.

Even at first glance nobody would have mistaken the animal for an ordinary domestic cat. She was a fat black kitten, but the jungle showed through in her every movement. Prowling her small enclosure restlessly, she looked like a tiny, tiny leopard cub. Mary said she ate and ate as long as a bit of food remained in sight. She seemed to thoroughly enjoy cuddling, and we each took turns holding her as Mary and I handled financial arrangements, instructions, and information on care and feeding.

When we arrived home, Gigi said, "Let me fix her a place to stay, please!" She received permission, and less than an hour later she called us in to see her handiwork. Under her desk she had placed a small rug. On it she spread a layer of chipped rock from the driveway and put in one of the large stones that bordered the drive. In one corner of the space spread several leafy branches from trees. She had arranged a towel so that it curtained the area into a dark, warm home.

"Gigi," I protested, "there isn't anything soft for her to rest on."

"Jungle cats rest on rocks," Gigi said confidently. "I've read about it."

Sure enough, Little Jag, as we named the kitten, proved the soundness of Gigi's ideas by draping herself over the large stone and looking perfectly comfortable.

As soon as we saw she was reasonably settled, we dropped the curtain in front of her simulated jungle den and closed the door to the bedroom. Minutes later a plaintive chirp came from the room.

"Oh!" I cried in alarm. "The canary is out of his cage and in that room. That kitty is small, but she'd eat a bird if she could catch one." I started for the bedroom, but Jimmy's voice halted me.

"Mamma, the canary is still in his cage. I see him," he said. "You heard something else."

I looked. Sure enough, the canary sat in his own place. Perhaps I'd heard a wild goldfinch outside. But no—there came that chirp again. This time I had no doubt about its coming from the bedroom. When I opened the door, out marched Little Jag, chirping away like a bird and letting us know that at times our company was preferable to her new lair.

Little Jag was a playful kitten, but her little teeth and claws were too sharp for comfort sometimes. She loved to climb up on the bed and chase our hands as we moved them about under the sheets. However, we never knew at what moment she'd tire of the game, turn swiftly, and bite our ears or nose. That would be painful, but it never kept anyone from playing with her. We would stroke her soft fur and were always pleased when we elicited her kettle-boiling purr, for she seldom favored us with it.

She ate and ate, but she played so long and so hard and kept so active that she didn't grow as fast as you'd expect from the amount of food she consumed. Her fur was so lustrous and thick that she seemed bursting with health and vitality.

For the next three weeks Little Jag went almost everywhere we did and was the center of attention. Everyone wanted to cuddle and hold her, to know what sort of animal she was, and all about her. In true feminine fashion she loved it all.

Then came summer camp. For several years I'd been camp nurse. This year the director had asked me to bring Little Jag along to provide something of interest to the campers. One hundred fifteen junior-age boys and girls can give one small jungle kitty a lot of attention. As I went about my duties in the medical building, I could look from my window and watch Little Jag bounding through the grass as she followed the children to camp council, crafts, and campfire. The campers were careful to ask my permission before picking her up. At mealtime, during swimming, and at rest period, Little Jag rested in the cage in which we'd brought her to camp. A group of interested youngsters always clustered around during her mealtimes. As the nights were cool, I filled a hot-water bottle and put it in the cage to keep her warm.

The only sick child I had at camp that year was a little boy who became ill the first evening at suppertime. Since I had known the child for some time and knew he had frequent stomach upsets, not until the next morning did I recognize his illness as intestinal flu. At once I isolated him on the sun porch of the medical building, away from contact with others, but where he could watch camp activity. Little Jag's cage was just inside the main room. Her antics provided plenty of entertainment for the sick boy. I carefully kept her away from him, however.

Friday afternoon the sick child had improved enough to move back to the boys' barracks. For the first time all week I felt I could sleep soundly at night without keeping one ear awake to listen for the needs of a patient. Therefore, when a moaning cry awakened me about daybreak, it bewildered me. It took a moment before I finally realized it was coming from Little Jag's cage. Even before I reached her, I knew she was desperately ill; and when I picked up her cold, limp little body, I felt sure it was too late.

I wrapped her in a towel, blew my warm breath on her, and tried to get some warm fluids down her throat, but she

81

was too deep in coma to swallow. Now and then she'd take a moaning breath. Forty-five minutes of such treatment exhausted me. Little Jag had gotten no better, but still I persisted. It was no use. An hour later she died. She had received the usual shots against cat diseases. The only reason I could imagine for her death was that she'd gotten the flu from the sick child.

It was a sad homecoming, with Little Jag's body wrapped in a towel in the cage in which she'd come so happily to camp. We buried her as soon as we reached home, and that same afternoon I called Mary's Pet Shop and ordered another jaguarundi. Mary told me she probably couldn't get another one that fall, but they'd be available again the following spring.

In late March Mary telephoned to say she had another jaguarundi kitten, but wasn't sure we'd want it. We'd specifically asked for a female, and the one that had arrived was a male.

Certainly different from Little Jag, he was one of the reddish-brown kind, called eyras. Some naturalists hold the opinion that they are not even jaguarundis, but a different species altogether. Longer, slinkier, and of a totally different disposition, the kitten reminded us only slightly of Little Jag.

We named him X-KE after the Jaguar sports car and called him Skee for short. Long of the opinion that females make better pets, to our considerable surprise we found that Skee was far gentler than Little Jag had been. Though Little Jag enjoyed cuddling, when she'd had enough, she'd stalk away to her lair. Skee just came back for more—and still more. He always sheathed his claws for our sakes, he bit gently, and his purr went full speed almost from morning till night.

He hated to have a door closed against him. A combination of rolling purr, whistling chirps, and anxious squeaks let us know his displeasure, as he batted his front paws against the offending door and waited for it to open. Only a hard heart indeed could resist such pleading.

His appetite was voracious. At the faintest whir of the electric can opener he'd come dashing into the kitchen, dance on his hind legs, and act as if his last meal—and a small one at that—had been served two weeks before. If the can contained something for the family's dinner, we would let him smell the lid, whereupon he would drop to all fours and calmly walk away. But if the can smelled of cat food, especially fish-flavored cat food, his dancing and purring and begging redoubled until one of us put his bowl before him and he could eat.

Casey, the Keeshond pup, thought Skee had been born to be his special playmate. At first they were about the same size and evenly matched. Their playing at times grew quite rough as one dragged the other about. In time, however, Casey grew bigger and stronger, and it seemed that Skee was in for some hard times. Several times we rescued him as Casey hauled him about, his whole head inside Casey's mouth. Each time he broke away from us and raced back to Casey to continue their rough play.

One day Casey came dashing up from the barn screaming as if he were being murdered. I thought that at the least one of the horses had stepped on him or kicked him. Running to see the cause of the outcry, I learned that he had been just a bit too hard on Skee, and Skee had turned on him with four sets of sharp claws and a mouthful of sharp teeth.

We left Skee with friends while we took vacation. On our return I went to get him. When I picked him up, he immediately jumped down and went back to the small girl who had been his playmate for the past three weeks. Retrieving him, I put him in the car and took him home, but if he remembered me, he showed no signs of it. Even after I put him down inside the house, he acted unhappy. Then Casey came trotting in. There followed a most joyous reunion, each nuzzling and licking the other in the most loving fashion. After that they had one of their old-time romps until we grew almost dizzy trying to watch their leaps and turns. When it ended, Skee came and sat on my lap to be cuddled, purring and chirping his pleasure at being home.

I'd received warnings, mostly from my husband, that someday Skee would show an interest in the birds. As time went by and Skee continued to ignore them, I grew complacent. One day, though, I heard the canary giving an odd little call. When I went to see what the trouble was, I found Skee sitting on the table, eyeing the canary from several feet away. Plainly his intentions were not honorable. The tip of his long tail twitched purposefully, and his mouth gaped wide open, displaying a full set of dangerous-looking teeth. Now and then he'd jerk his lower jaw sharply upward, never quite closing his mouth. He acted as if he intended to scare the poor bird to death to save the trouble of killing it. I scolded Skee and moved the table so that he couldn't reach the canary if he did decide to jump. Several times after that I heard the canary's call for help and came to find Skee eyeing him.

Then came the day when it was Butch yelling for help. His alarmed squawks brought me on the run, for I had an idea what was bothering him. Sure enough, Skee lay sprawled across the top of Butch's cage, one lightning-fast paw striking at the yelling, terrorized bird. I spanked and scolded Skee and sent him from the room in disgrace. After giving the situation some thought, I decided to see if more food would turn Skee's attention from the birds. Apparently it did, for as long as he had food available, he paid no attention to Butch, George, and the canary. The canary's cry for help is often the first indication that Skee thinks it is mealtime.

Skee shows no fear of any other animal—only a wary caution around strange dogs. Occasionally he and "THAT COATI!" have a sparring match, both hissing and squeaking, but neither hurts the other. Sometimes they chase each other around a bit in a free-for-all, but there is not the friendship between them that exists between Skee and Casey.

Skee is full-grown now, about the size of an ordinary domestic cat. Still gentle, he loves to bound out from underneath some piece of furniture and grab an unsuspecting passerby with his paws. But since he carefully keeps his claws sheathed, he has never snagged any woman's nylons. He purrs as happily and as often as when he was a tiny kitten and loves to be wherever the rest of the family is.

He occasionally accompanies the children on a walk through the fields, catching grasshoppers and an occasional mouse; but so far he has shown no tendency to revert to the wild. His greatest joy seems to lie in stretching out under the couch with only his head out, his bright brown eyes watching everything going on within his sight, deciding who shall be the victim of his next playful pounce.

Mud and Ape

I was trying to coax to me the little baby monkey that
had the run of the zoo, and though he showed interest, I
had not yet succeeded in getting him to perch on my arm.
He had allowed me to pet him before, but for some reason,
that day he chose to be capricious. The zoo was almost deserted at that early afternoon hour. I had no competitors
for his attention. Still, he disdained my offered hand, choos-
ing instead to tease the guinea pigs, swing perilously close

to the big multicolored macaws, or run teasingly by me while ignoring my overtures of friendship.

One of the animal keepers, a friend of mine, walked up and said casually, "How would you like to have a monkey?"

I hesitated. I wasn't really sure I would like a monkey for a pet. Once we'd had one, and after that I'd been certain I'd never want another.

Jimmy had informed us one year that he wanted a pet for Christmas—a monkey, if possible. Mary had a small squirrel monkey in her shop which she promised to save for me until Christmas Eve. His price included the cage, for which I felt truly grateful, as I'd not yet grown brave enough to try to make my own. So on Christmas Eve we brought the little monkey home, tied a big red bow on top of his cage, and put him in the warm garage until the next day.

Christmas morning we presented the monkey to Jimmy, who almost ignored all his other presents. To tell the truth, so did all the rest of us. My husband held out his hand to the little animal, which promptly bit him. "Listen, young fellow," I scolded the monkey, "if you act like that, your name is going to be mud around here!"

"Oh, is that his name, Mamma?" someone exclaimed.

"Is *what* his name?" I asked.

"Mud! You said his name would be Mud."

"Yes, his name is Mud," insisted Jimmy. "That's what I'm going to call him."

Thus Mud received his name, and it fit. He had a terrible temper and used his teeth indiscriminately on young and old alike. There seemed never to be a time when some member of the family wasn't nursing the marks of Mud's displeasure.

But we had another complaint against Mud. No matter

how often we cleaned his cage, it smelled bad within half an hour. Ordinarily we cleaned our caged animals at least once a day, putting in clean newspapers when we replenished the food and water supply. Then once a week in winter and twice a week in summer, we put the animal into a smaller cage while we thoroughly scrubbed his regular one and left it to dry in the sun. Such a routine not only helps keep down odors, but contributes greatly to the health of the animals. But all the cleaning we did had no effect on Mud. His cage still smelled bad.

Worst of all, Mud refused, absolutely refused, to be a pet. He didn't want anyone to cuddle, stroke, or even hold him. Furthermore, he took fiendish delight in outwitting us —he always considered it a red-letter day whenever he managed to get out of his cage. His objective seemed to be to stay out as long as possible and to see how many people he could bite during his capture. In the beginning, we managed to trick Mud back into the cage, but that didn't last for long. To give him his due, he was intelligent and never fell for the same ruse twice. When we ran out of new tricks, we had to rely on strength of numbers; and even so, it was no short or easy task to catch him. Eventually we, too, got smart and learned to check and double-check the fastenings on the cage door each time we closed it. But by that time we had paid a steep price for the lesson.

The day came when Mud finally and irrevocably branded himself with the mark of Cain. I returned home from an errand to find the monkey skipping about the sun porch with the mutilated body of Sunshine, my canary, mutely testifying to the fact of murder. Mud had not killed because of hunger—that I could have understood. He had killed wantonly, without any reason that we could see. From that time on, we only tolerated him. We fed, watered, and cleaned him faithfully, but without interest. And when one day we found him dead on the floor of his cage, one hand still in his feeding dish, nobody mourned. With a sense of guilty relief we removed his smelly cage, cleaned it, and put it away until the day we had a more lovable occupant for it.

So when the animal keeper asked me, "Would you like to have a monkey?" I thought of Mud, even as my incorrigible optimism began gathering arguments as to why I probably *would* like to have a monkey. So I looked the animal keeper right in the eye and, with only minimal hesitation, answered, "Yes, I believe I would."

"Fine," he responded. "I have one I'll give you."

"You—you can't mean this one?" I queried hopefully, indicating the little fellow that even at that moment had finally jumped onto my shoulder, and now began rifling my pocket for sweets.

"No," the keeper said, smiling. "Not Toby. But you wouldn't want Toby, anyway. He's cute, but he'd never be the pet you want. He's too active, never still enough to let anyone hold him and play with him. Come over here, and I'll show you the one I mean."

In a cage on the other side of the building a number of monkeys clung to the bars. Though some were brown and others were black, all had the same shape and color pattern —dark bodies with a lighter ring around the face and half-way back on the head.

"These are ringtails, capuchin monkeys," explained my friend. "They are the ones organ grinders use because of their intelligence." He pointed to a black one perched near the bottom of the bars. "That's Pee-Wee, the one we'll let you have. You see, after Pee-Wee's birth, we left him with his mother instead of taking him away and hand-rearing him, as we often do the babies born here in the zoo. As a result, he got rickets. By the time we realized the trouble, it had permanently crippled him. He gets around fine, doesn't seem to be at all bothered by it, but his hind legs are both deformed, and he doesn't use one of them very much. He isn't a good exhibit at all—people think we haven't taken care of him. We've been looking for a nice home for him. I know you'll enjoy him and take good care of him."

"Is he tame?" I queried.

"I don't know," he answered. "He's never been handled, but he seems like a gentle little fellow. I don't think you'll have any trouble on that score. I'll get a net and catch him and see how he acts."

As he endeavored to catch Pee-Wee with the net, every monkey in the cage fled six different directions at once, screaming hysterically. Those in the adjacent cages joined the bedlam, and then those across the building added their voices, until the building fairly vibrated with monkey shrieks. Even after we caught Pee-Wee and he lay fearfully in the keeper's arms with his mouth pursed into diamond shape and his voice subsided to a whimpering, "Oh! Oh! Oh! Oh!" the other monkeys kept up their racket for several minutes before they, too, quieted down.

Within hours after getting him home, we rechristened Pee-Wee. Because of his tendency to cry, "Oh! Oh! Oh!" so pitifully, as if he thought we had obtained him as the main course for our next meal, we reversed the syllables, and he became Weepy.

The next day I let Weepy out of the cage. He swung along the floor, cautiously exploring, then climbed the drapes and sat watching from that vantage point.

When he came down to eat, I decided it was time to put him back into his cage. He had other ideas. Finally I cornered him in the bathroom. He swung down into the tub, curled himself into a little ball, and whimpered fearfully when I picked him up, but showed no inclination to bite. Several times that day I let him out, each time having to pick him up out of the bathtub. Each time I played with him and cuddled him a few minutes before putting him back into his cage.

The following day he never bothered to try to get into the tub whenever I wanted to pick him up. He just curled up wherever he happened to be and let me get him. The day after that, to my joy, as I approached Weepy, he held up his arms just like a baby that wants an adult to pick him up. Later that day he came over and climbed up on my lap as I sat reading. The metamorphosis from unhandled exhibit to trusting pet had taken only three days.

Soon the name Weepy was no longer appropriate, for he stopped his "Oh! Oh! Oh!" cry whenever we came near. At first in fun, then as a matter of habit, the children began referring to him as Ape, and Ape he remained.

Ape loved women and girls, tolerated little boys, and actively disliked or distrusted men. The bigger the man, the more Ape abhorred him. Two of my sons stand close to six feet tall. Ape showed them how he felt, and they reacted characteristically. Ray ignored or teased Ape and earned his further dislike. Don spent hours coaxing and cajoling and at times got rewarded with some of the crumbs of Ape's affection.

But my husband incurred Ape's wrath most often—daily, in fact. Ape took offense at my husband's kissing me every morning when he left for the office, and greeting me with the same when he returned in the evening. This, Ape did not like at all. If Ape was in his cage, he made a shrill scream of anger. If loose, he would make futile little rushes at my husband, showing his teeth and gibbering with rage. Whether his displays resulted from jealousy or from honest concern for my welfare, I never found out. The fact that I always emerged unharmed from such encounters should have reassured Ape somewhat, but it never seemed to do so.

Ape intrigued most men, and they tried to make friends with him, only to be rebuffed. One day at a florist shop one of the owners tried long and patiently to win Ape's approval, but to no avail. "He doesn't seem to like men," I explained. "I've never yet seen him show even any tolerance for one." At that moment the man's son-in-law came in. Immediately Ape left me and went to the second man, grinning, chattering, hugging his arm, and showing the warmest affection for him, while I stared. He'd made me a liar, but I was too astonished to feel resentful. It was the only time I ever saw Ape show the slightest regard for a man.

Ape never showed any jealousy of the other animals. Many times "THAT COATI!," Skee, and Ape shared my lap peacefully.

All children seem to love monkeys, and they made Ape an object of attention wherever we went. If I left him in the car, on my return I'd find it surrounded with children and some persons not quite so young. He was gentle and usually docile, but seemed frightened of the tiniest children and never allowed them to hold him.

During Vacation Bible School, its directors asked me to help by bringing an animal a day for the nature study. On the day I took Ape, a photographer from a local newspaper came in and took pictures of the children as they played with the monkey. When she learned that I had other animals, she asked if she could see them someday. I told her I'd be glad for her to come anytime. The pictures of Ape and the children turned out nicely, and as a result our Vacation Bible School got more publicity than any other in town.

Two weeks later the photographer called to ask if I minded if she interviewed and photographed me with my pets for the newspaper. I didn't mind, so we set a day for her to stop by. Then the day before the interview Ape pulled a trick that left him in the doghouse for some time.

While we were out working in the garden, Ape turned on the cold water faucet at the kitchen sink with the drain closed. When we returned to the house, we found the place awash—water all over the kitchen and dining room, seeping into the living room carpet, and running down the basement stairs. Ape sat high and dry on the kitchen table, watching wide-eyed as we shut off the water and grabbed brooms, mops, sponges, and anything else at hand to get rid of the water.

When we told our photographer friend about it the next day, she found it highly amusing. The next week's paper featured a picture of Ape looking penitent, and the caption read, "Aw, fellas, I didn't mean to do it!" Of course the article included a picture of Skee and "THAT COATI!" but Ape was the star.

The summer kept getting hotter and hotter. One day the temperature reached 110 degrees at our house. The next morning when I got up, I called Ape as usual and received no reply, which was *not* usual. I went to investigate and found Ape sick.

I coaxed him into taking a little bit of food and water, and then took him to the animal hospital, where he received an antibiotic injection. On the way home I stopped at the grocery store to buy some grapes, hoping to tempt his appetite with them. While I was still inside, Gigi came in to tell me Ape was acting odd.

I hurried out to see—and he certainly was. His face had flushed a mottled red, and his breathing made grunting sounds. I called the doctor from the store, and he said to return right away. So back we hurried as fast as we legally could. Ape received an injection the minute we walked into the animal hospital, and in a few minutes the alarming symptoms vanished. Ape had been allergic to the antibiotics.

Ape was still alive the next morning, but refused food and water, wanting only to be held. About midmorning he died. He had been with us only five months, but he left years of empty places in our hearts.

T-Bird

Shortly after Ape's death I decided to get another monkey. The question was, Should I get another ringtail like Ape, or should I get some other kind?

I knew a taxi driver who owned an ocelot named Tabu. He and I met now and then at Mary's Pet Shop, and he seemed knowledgeable about animals. I'd heard him talk about a pet woolly monkey he'd once had. He spoke of the woolly's gentleness and intelligence, what good pets these monkeys made, and how lovable and affectionate they could be.

Although I read about the different kinds of monkeys in the animal books I had, until I got to Mary's I still hadn't made up my mind. Mary highly recommended a woolly, so I placed an order for one.

The next day all the airlines went on strike, and since the suppliers ship monkeys only by air, I had to wait—and wait—and wait. When the strike ended, the civilian shipments had to wait until the government priority goods got moved. Thus nearly three months passed before Mary called to say my monkey had arrived.

In my reading I'd learned that woolly monkeys are either brown or dark gray. Somehow I got the idea that the brown ones were rare, and so, expecting a gray one, I picked out the name "Shadow."

At the pet shop Mary indicated the cage which housed my new pet. I peeked in. Two tiny baby monkeys, tightly locked in each other's arms, crouched in one corner. The minute I opened the cage door, one little fellow leaped out and grabbed me tightly around the neck. The other one ran fearfully as far away as he could get.

"Mary, is this one mine?" I asked, indicating the little fellow holding onto my neck.

"Yes, that's your woolly." Mary smiled. "The other is a little ringtail."

The little woolly abruptly deserted me and went to my son Jimmy, who wore a red plaid shirt. (As we got to know him better, we felt his preference for the color red seemed more than just a coincidence.) While he perched on Jimmy's shoulder, I could see him better. He was a most appealing little animal with a round head, big eyes, and dense brown fur. The soles of his feet looked like soft black leather, and the last few inches of his tail were bare on the underside to match his feet. Seeing his color, I knew I'd have to pick out another name for him.

We named him T-Bird, keeping to the sports car motif we'd begun with Skee.

Acquaintances had told me that when a woolly wants to express affection for someone, he puts his head against that person's face or hair, shakes his head rapidly back and forth, and gives a series of little chuckly grunts. Some say that is how he laughs. Before he had been in our home two hours, the little monkey had performed the ritual with each member of the family.

I also learned that woolly monkeys can scream louder than nearly any other monkey, and that the mothers carry their babies until they are almost a year old. T-Bird was only two months old when we got him, and he expected me to take his mother's place, letting him ride on my shoulder most of the day. He screamed wrathfully whenever I pried him loose and put him back in the cage.

T-Bird acted in many ways much like a human baby. He got hiccups, and we had to give him a drink of water in order for him to get over them.

He would go through his headshaking, grunting laugh whenever someone tickled his fat tummy or the bottom of his feet. And one night, after he'd eaten more than usual, he cried like a colicky baby. Just as I would have treated a human child, I burped him, after which he settled down and went to sleep.

Though he was quite adept at swinging on the drapes, climbing on sticks, and doing acrobatics on our hands, he still hadn't learned to jump from one place to another properly. Time after time he would jump from the back of the couch onto the cushion, or from my hand onto the bed.

Each time he'd land all sprawled out like a child doing a belly flopper, staying in that position until someone picked him up and petted him and told him what a smart fellow he was. Then he'd try again.

When I took a rest in the afternoon, he would curl up on my back for a nap, and woe to me if I wanted to change position. Each move I made, he met with a stream of indignant monkey chatter. After finishing his nap, he'd get up and walk around on his hind legs, often with his prehensile tail curled around one wrist.

Any unexpected noise or any move I then made sent him flying back to his perch on my shoulder with both arms, and frequently his tail, too, tightly wrapped around my neck. In order to get him off, I had to pull him loose. The minute I began to pry, he began to cry, until by the time I had him loose, he had worked up a full-fledged ear-splitting scream.

Later I learned to sit on the couch and wait until he got down and began to play. Then I'd swoop down and pick him up, holding him high so he couldn't get a grip on my clothing. The noise was the same, but it involved far less trouble.

One day when I was in a hurry and T-Bird was more reluctant than usual to leave his accustomed place, I put my coat on and left him there on my shoulder. Within a few minutes he cautiously poked his head above my coat collar. Since my collar is black fur, he was nearly impossible to see. Since that day he has accompanied me many places.

Of course, sometimes people spot him, and then he gets lots of attention. One young grocery clerk smothered a scream with her hand, then exclaimed, "Hey, he's alive!"

"Yes," I smilingly agreed, "he certainly is."

"I thought he was just part of your fur," she said, "and then he winked at me!"

Another grocery clerk thought her eyes were playing

tricks on her when a small black hand reached out from my collar and picked up a grape from the sack she was weighing for me.

At home I had to watch T-Bird closely because everything he picked up went into his mouth. We had some real struggles when I saw him munching something and had to remove it from his mouth to see whether or not it was harmful. Usually it turned out to be nothing worse than a piece of paper, but he never let me investigate without putting up a fight.

His appetite was prodigious and indiscriminate. We learned early not to let him out during mealtime. A person had to be fast indeed to get a spoonful of food into his mouth if T-Bird sat perched on his shoulder, for the monkey could scoop a handful of food off a spoon and have it eaten before the holder of the spoon got it to his mouth. He particularly attacked anyone who ate mashed potatoes. Apples were one of his favorite fruits. Anyone who ate one in his presence without offering him some would soon find a little woolly face close to his own as T-Bird helped himself to a bite. If given a slice of apple, he held it in both hands and ate it as one would a slice of watermelon, discarding the skin when he came to it. Whatever food came in sight, T-Bird stretched his hands toward it while he begged for it with pleading little chirps.

The individual in charge of the MV program one week asked me to give the Nature Nugget. When I inquired if I could bring T-Bird, she told me that was just the sort of thing the Nature Nugget should be. So on Sabbath afternoon T-Bird and I appeared before the congregation. I had feared that he might be shy and cling like a limpet to the back of my neck where no one could see him, and then unleash one of his unearthly screams if I tried to move him into sight of the people. Instead, he sat upright on my shoulder with one arm around my head, regarding the members of the audience with as much interest as they showed in watching him. Then spying the microphone, he eased close and peered at it intently. Finally he reached out and patted it. The pats came over the loudspeaker as a series of loud pops, whereupon he fled back to my shoulder. He sat quite still during most of the talk. Then when I picked up the end of his tail and wrapped it around my finger to demonstrate how he used it, he stretched out a hand and pulled his tail back and curled it carefully back around my neck, where he seemed to think it belonged.

After the service we went back to the foyer of the church, where everyone had a chance to see him at close range. He made many friends among the children, though I'm not sure of the reactions of the parents when their children told them they wanted a monkey "just like T-Bird" for Christmas.

Later someone asked me to have the Week of Prayer for the second graders in the local church school. I planned lessons around my pets. The first morning I took Butch and talked to the children about being careful in speech. The myna bird delighted us all by talking for the children, something he seldom does for strangers.

The next morning I spoke about my canary, Caruso, who, though he has only one talent, that of singing, uses it all day long.

On Friday I took T-Bird. I told the children about the three monkeys I had had—Mud, who had been so mean nobody really loved him; Ape, who had been so sweet everybody loved him; and T-Bird, who was good most of the time, but his screaming marred his sweetness. Then I took T-Bird around the room so that the children could pet him, but the sight of so many little hands reaching out for him frightened him and he cried pitifully. After that they had to be content with just looking at him.

Friends had warned me that baby woollys were prone to illnesses and hard to raise. When an epidemic of intestinal flu hit our community and reached our family, I worried that T-Bird might get it; but while the rest of us came down sick for one or two days each, T-Bird stayed well. Not happy, but well; for I had forbidden the family to hold him during the epidemic, and he missed all the attention he had grown accustomed to. My friend at the zoo told me he thought that baby monkeys who got plenty of love and attention had more resistance to disease, and that may have been why T-Bird escaped sickness that time.

Then a few weeks later he developed a cold and cough. At the animal hospital he received an injection of penicillin, and the veterinarian told me to give him half a penicillin tablet twice daily for five days. I had to dissolve the medicine in a hypodermic syringe without the needle, hold his mouth open, and squirt it in. He hated it and made the most ferocious faces as he tried to avoid swallowing, but twenty years as a nurse had taught me a few tricks about giving medicine to reluctant patients. The penicillin went down. The cold disappeared, and T-Bird was happy to have the medication discontinued.

At times I took T-Bird when I went up to my husband's clinic. One day in particular stands out. A little three-year-old girl was so frightened that her mother was having trouble keeping her still while my husband tried to examine her ears. Knowing T-Bird and I were in the building, he came and brought us to the examining room. Within minutes T-Bird's antics so enthralled the little girl that she submitted to the examination without a second thought.

101

T-Bird had his favorites among the clinic employees and always showed his happiness at seeing them again, holding out his hands for them to take him and giving them his special headshaking greeting. Their calling themselves "Aunt Zella" or "Aunt Janice" in speaking to him or saying, "Here, go back to your mother," when they gave him back to me, continually amused me.

T-Bird's greatest and most surprising conquest was my mother-in-law. She had always shown at least some interest in our pets, but none won her heart as T-Bird did. When he put his arms about her head and buried his face in her lovely white hair, she was captivated. From then on, whenever she came in the door, T-Bird was sure of a welcoming shoulder and hours of loving attention. She confessed rather shyly that monkeys had always fascinated her, but she had never had the opportunity to play with one before.

Unlike Ape, T-Bird is as fond of men as he is of women. Particularly, he loves my husband. When I kiss my husband good-bye in the morning, so does T-Bird, though my husband says he thinks the animal is only sampling the flavor of his after-shave lotion.

One day I decided to buy T-Bird some toys. Thinking that a woolly Teddy bear might make him more agreeable to spending his time in his cage, I bought that first. A rattle and a rubber ball came next. He was afraid of the bear and the rattle, and ignored the ball. I persisted, however, until he got used to the bear, and then became rather fond of it. Unfortunately, Skee also wanted the bear and was constantly snatching it and running off under the bed with it. We had to rescue it quickly, for Skee was rough with stuffed toys and always tore them to pieces and left bits of stuffing all over the house. But he was persistent, too. If someone safely put the bear up on a closet shelf, Skee sat alertly by the closet door until someone opened it, and then the animal jumped repeatedly, but futilely, trying to grab the toy. If T-Bird was playing on the couch with the bear, Skee would skulk along, biding his time until the bear once more fell into his possession. At last his patience earned its reward—he got the bear one day when nobody was watching and tore it completely to pieces.

T-Bird's next toy was a little rubber doll, resplendent with orange nylon braids. He played with it happily by the hour. But it, too, drew covetous eyes. Nearly every little girl who came into the house noticed the doll in the monkey cage and removed it, ostensibly to give it a bath, then to play with it, until eventually it disappeared.

T-Bird never seems to miss his toys. After all, he has little plastic measuring cups to play with, and magazines and papers to tear into strips. There are drape pulls to swing on and broomsticks to climb. What more would a little monkey need?

Sugar and Eagle

The Pathfinder Council meeting was just breaking up when someone called me to the phone. I heard the voice of the receptionist at my husband's clinic on the line. "Mrs. Norman, your husband wants you to stop at the drugstore on the way home and get two baby bottles with nipples."

"Baby bottles?" I repeated blankly. "What for?"

"He wants them for some little lambs, he said."

"Little lambs? You mean—lambs, like sheep?"

"Yes, I suppose so."

"There weren't any little lambs at my house when I left to come to this meeting this evening," I said. "Have you seen any up at the office?"

"N-no," she replied. "Dr. Norman said they were out in his car, and he's going to take them home right away."

"Well, all right," I commented doubtfully. "I'll get the bottles, but I'll bet he's playing a trick of some kind."

I went to get my coat, but before I could get out the door, I had another phone call—this time from Raymond. "Mother, do you know what? Daddy is bringing home two little lambs for us," he announced excitedly, "and we want you to——"

"—stop at the drugstore and get two baby bottles and nipples," I finished for him.

"How did you know what we wanted?"

"Lambs have to be fed, don't they?" I countered.

"Yes, and please hurry," he said. "They're hungry, for daddy said so."

"Just a minute, Ray, before you hang up," I said. "Where did they come from?"

"From that man out in the country that has all the sheep. You remember—he said if he had any orphan sheep, he'd let us have one to raise, only he had two of them."

Now I remembered. We had gone for a ride in the country, and the children had spied a flock of sheep with their little lambs. My husband had recognized the name on the mailbox as that belonging to a patient of his, so we drove into the farmyard. The young farmer was home and was more than willing to take us around and show us his sheep.

The antics of the lambs captivated the children and, to be truthful, enthralled the parents nearly as much.

Few baby animals are as cute as lambs, and those were

105

typical. They would take off at a dead run, leaping, skipping, skyrocketing along almost to the fence. Then they would put on their brakes with forefeet outstretched, pivot, run back to their mothers, and stand still for a breathing spell. A few moments later they would do it all over again. We could hardly tear ourselves away to go into the barn to see the lambs born that day.

The barn contained five babies less than twenty-four hours old. All the lambs were white with black heads. The tiny little fellows looked as if they'd sniffed around in the dirt and had forgotten to wash their faces afterward.

In one of the stalls lay a sick ewe, whose lamb the farmer kept in the house and fed by bottle. He said he had to raise several lambs that way every lambing season.

Finally, after two delightful hours, we had to go. The farmer walked to the car with us. To comfort the reluctant-to-leave children, who dragged their feet and looked back for a last glimpse of the lambs, he said, "If I have any more orphan lambs, would you like to have one to raise?"

"Oh, yes! Yes!" they all agreed loudly.

"That is, if your parents don't mind," he amended hastily.

I quickly convinced him I'd like that, too.

But that had been last spring, and now it was fall. No wonder I had forgotten.

Recalling Ray's plea for speed because the lambs were hungry, I got the requested equipment and hurried home. The children had a pan of milk already warm. While I filled the bottles, they held the lambs, and then told me about them as the little fellows ate.

The lambs had already received names during the less-than-half-an-hour they had been in the house.

"This one is Sugar," Ray said.

106

"Because he's so sweet and cuddly," Gigi explained.

"And the other one is Eagle. See that spot on his head?" Ray added. "It's shaped like an eagle, don't you think?"

"Well-l-l," I hedged. If I shut one eye and stretched my imagination to the limit, and then took Ray's word for it, maybe that spot did faintly resemble an eagle in shape. But what did it really matter? Eagle was as good a name as any for a sheep.

Eagle finished his bottle and eyed Sugar's with interest, crowding against him and trying to get the last few drops. Ray picked up the greedy little fellow, and I suddenly noticed a rubber band around the lamb's tail.

"Who put that rubber band on his tail?" I demanded.

"The farmer did, Mamma," Ray said. "Daddy told me. He says the rubber band cuts off the circulation and makes the tails fall off before long. It doesn't hurt as much or bleed as it would if you cut them off."

"Well, it sounds reasonable," I commented.

"They don't act as if it hurts them any," Ray remarked.

"No," I agreed. "Did daddy say how old they are?"

"I think he said they were born this morning."

"I don't suppose he told you how often they need feeding, did he?"

"I think—I think he said every three or four hours, but I'm not sure. Daddy just brought them home and stayed a few minutes. Then he had to go to the hospital. But I think he said to feed them every three or four hours."

"Oh, oh!" I said to myself. "Here I go back on the old night shift. I thought I had left that for good when Danny Joe quit using a bottle four years ago."

It really wasn't so bad. It was just past one o'clock in the morning when I heard their plaintive "Baa-a-a" and got up to feed them. They butted and nudged me while the milk warmed, and then they drank so fast they hardly took time to breathe. All the time their tails wagged frantically back and forth. They were so cute and lovable that I spent an extra quarter of an hour playing with them before going back to bed. At five-thirty I got up and fed them again.

They lost their tails as predicted about a week later. Not too long after that they began to sleep all night without the early morning feeding.

Sugar and Eagle played in the house as we'd seen the other lambs romp in the field. They loved to run up the stairs. I'd hear them start from the basement, clackety-clack up the basement stairs, clippety-clip on the kitchen linoleum, thumpety-thump across the dining-room and living-room carpets, clackety-clack up the stairs to the second story, and down to the end of the hall. A pause—and then the whole thing reversed—back to the stairs and down, through the living and dining rooms, across the kitchen, and back down the basement stairs. Over and over they repeated it until they dropped breathless in the living room, where I sat or worked.

At other times they played tag. Apparently I served as home base, for the one being chased sooner or later came dashing in and jumped up on my lap, closely followed by his pursuer. They would settle down there to let me pet them for a while, then away they'd go again.

On mild winter days we'd let them outside in the yard. I kept close watch on them from the window, for I didn't want them to stray away. They would run and leap about all over the lawn, afterward lying down to rest. Then suddenly, as if jerked by strings, they'd jump up and race madly to the front door, pawing at it with their black hooves and bleating as desperately as if starvation imminently threatened them.

As they grew older, their appetites increased beyond one bottle of milk at a feeding. While I filled the bottles a second time, they would push and poke at me with their heads, all the while complaining noisily that they were still famished. Whichever one finished first tried to butt his brother away and take what remained in his bottle.

The bigger they grew, the harder it became for me to stand upright and fill their bottles while they butted and nudged me. I decided that they needed to learn to drink their milk out of a pan. Before they did so, we spilled a lot of milk over both the lambs and me, but learn they did. And as before, each one tried to finish his milk first in order to push his brother away and snatch his. Feeding them in a common pan was not the answer, either, for they kept butting at each other and invariably spilled all the milk. Finally I had to put them in separate rooms.

The older and bigger they got, the more problems the lambs presented. They could jump to the top of almost any piece of furniture in the house. They made twice as much noise now as they ran from the basement to the second story, and I enjoyed their games of tag less and less. There is something disconcerting, to say the least, at having two sharp-hooved thirty-five-pound missiles landing in your lap, one right after the other. Plainly we couldn't keep them in the house much longer, and we couldn't afford to have the yard fenced tight enough to let them run loose there.

At last we decided to give them back to the farmer. We were going on a short trip during the children's spring vacation from school, and that seemed a logical time to part with Sugar and Eagle. We'd not have to worry about getting someone to care for them while we were gone, and the trip would prove enough of a distraction for the children to keep them from mourning too much over losing their lambs.

So one day the farmer came and put Sugar and Eagle into his panel truck and drove away, and the next morning we started on our trip.

About ten days after our return, my husband came home from the clinic chuckling. "That young fellow was in the office today. You know—the one we got the lambs from," he said.

"Yes?" I prompted.

"He wanted to know how we trained those lambs to jump. He said that no matter where he puts them, they jump the fence and go pounding up to the house, bawling for someone to let them in!"

I laughed at the picture his words brought to my mind. "What's he doing about them?" I asked.

"I think he's keeping them in the barn for now," he answered. "I told him how they used to jump up on the furniture and run up and down stairs. He said he guessed that explained it."

A week later we drove out to the farm for a short visit. A group of half-grown lambs came running pell-mell at the fence, but when the others ran back, two of them stopped, then turned to face us. One was sweet and cuddly, and the other had a spot on his head that was unmistakably shaped like an eagle. They took a few hesitant steps toward us, but then, realizing that the rest of the lambs had gone in the other direction, they turned and with mighty bounds ran to catch up.

Cookie

The cacophony of assorted noises blared at us from the State Fair Midway. I was tired, the children were fussy—it was time to go home. We had gone through the great barns which housed the exhibitions of cows, horses, sheep, pigs, and other animals; we had seen the sewing and canning handiwork of the 4-H girls; we had admired the purple-, blue-, and red-ribbon winners among the farm produce; we had taken one turn around the Midway at the children's request. Now it was time to get them home and into bed.

Then my husband pointed out a small tent whose sign advertised an exhibit of snakes. "Shall we go in?" he asked. "It's only a dime."

"We may as well." I sighed. "Snakes are the only things I've not seen today."

I don't remember anything about the snakes. What I do remember is a small catlike animal in a cage nearby. When I expressed an interest, the man in charge took her out and stroked her as he told me about her. He said she was a cacomistle, or ring-tailed cat, and that such cats made good pets. Her large eyes identified her as a nocturnal animal. She had a pointed face and proportionately oversized ears. Her tail was fluffy and ringed like a raccoon's. I thought she was beautiful, and I wanted one like her. So did my husband!

At home I got out the encyclopedia. Cacomistles, so it said, were also known as miners' cats, because of their habit of moving into prospectors' cabins and keeping the mouse population under control. As I had suspected, scientists considered them members of the raccoon family. They lived in the southwestern United States and southward.

For the next eight years I tried over and over to locate a cacomistle for sale. I even wrote to friends in the Southwest to see if they could find one for me. Finally I learned of Mary's Pet Shop. One day I asked her about it, little dreaming she could help me. I'd never found a pet shop owner who'd ever heard of a cacomistle and had never found a zoo that had one. But Mary's resourcefulness surprised me. She'd never heard of a cacomistle, either, but she was willing to contact all the animal dealers she knew to see if she could locate one.

Finally a dealer in California wrote that he'd send one when it was available. Almost a year went by.

Then one afternoon Mary called. "Your cacomistle is being shipped from California this afternoon," she said. "You should be able to come over and see it tomorrow."

I could hardly believe it. It seemed too good to be true. And, as it turned out, it was.

About three hours later another phone call came from Mary. "Mrs. Norman, I have bad news," she said. "Your cacomistle won't be arriving after all. When the dealer took him to the vet to have his shots, and mentioned he was sending him to Nebraska, the vet informed him that it was against the law to send cacomistles out of California. I'm going to try to get one sent up from South America through a dealer in Florida."

Then another year went by without my hearing any more about a cacomistle. Ten years had passed since I'd first seen the one at the State Fair. But one day I stopped by Mary's, and she said, "Your cacomistle is here. I've been keeping him until I was sure he was healthy before I called you. He's been here five days now, so you may take him if you want to."

This time I had to believe it was true, for there paced *my* cacomistle in a cage right before my eyes. He looked just like the one I remembered except that he was just about half as big, being younger. He hissed and spat furiously when Mary put on heavy gloves and picked him up to put him in a box for the trip home. Mary said she felt sure I'd have no trouble taming him into the pet I wanted, and I felt quite confident, too.

The first thing he did when I got him home was to bite me. That's how I learned how sharp his teeth were. I kept him in an old cage that had once housed a myna bird while I built him one just like the cage I had built for the coati. After I finished it, he went in willingly enough and settled

113

himself on the platform I had put inside for him. But he viewed the world from there with a decidedly jaundiced eye. When I went to put food inside for him, I moved fast enough to keep from getting bitten, but his teeth left a definite groove in one of my fingernails.

Cookie—we had selected his name years before—acted not so much vicious as frightened. Each time I approached the cage, he would spring at me, hissing and spitting. His tail would fluff up, the hair at the back of his neck stood on end, and you could see how his heart hammered against his ribs. If I put my hand easily and gently against the wire of the cage, he would slowly edge up to it and sniff at it, then go back and settle down. Before long he would take food from my hand, but he seemed uneasy about it.

One morning Cookie wasn't in his cage. We found him flattened between the cage and the wall, a space of not more than two inches. It was no easy matter to get him back inside his cage, but finally we forced him to go in. Nearly every morning after that we found that he had managed to escape. It got so we would let him have the run of the house during the day and then battle him back into the cage at night.

During the daylight hours he'd curl up on a windowsill or under the couch to sleep. Toward evening he'd come out to play. It was a joy to see him scamper up the drapes, run along the top and down the other side to a windowsill, and there peek at us through the center opening. He was sure-footed and graceful.

Sometimes if he hid under the couch, Gigi would roll a ball of crumpled paper at him and he'd bat it back with a paw. Other times she would stretch out quietly on the floor without moving, and Cookie would come and pat her hand with his paw, or walk across her body. He never favored any of the rest of us with such little attentions.

At night when it came time for him to go into his cage, it would be either an all-out effort or a simple matter, depending on who was in charge. For several nights my husband chased him with a broom and forced him back inside. Thereafter all he had to do was point to the cage door, and Cookie went inside with all speed. But Cookie realized the rest of us were too softhearted to use a broom on him, so he made us work for every inch as he retreated finally to the cage.

Then one morning Cookie escaped from his cage, and we could find him nowhere. All day we looked for him. The next day we discovered him in the basement workroom. Because of the many places he could hide, he managed to stay loose in the room for several weeks. We put his cage in the room and put his food and water in it, hoping that sometime while he was eating, one of us would happen by and be able to close the door. But no matter how fast we were, Cookie was faster. The minute we touched the door of his cage, he sprang out and away like the proverbial streak of lightning.

For some time we didn't know where he slept, but one day I happened to open a drawer to take out some sewing materials and saw Cookie blinking up at me. Almost at once he jumped up and ran under the stairs, where we stored several boxes. Later we found him sleeping on the top shelf of a built-in cupboard. He slept there for at least two weeks.

We noticed that while he was out of the cage, he seemed far less fearful of us, coming readily to take food from our hands. I voted to leave him out of the cage, in hopes I could tame him easier, but my husband outvoted me. One evening with his trusty broom in hand he chased Cookie back into the cage.

Then he gave me an ultimatum. Within six months I had

to have Cookie well tamed, or else donate him to the local zoo. I had tried hard before, but now I redoubled my efforts. I "baby-talked" to him by the half hour, I offered my hand for him to sniff, I fed him his favorite dried figs, and tried over and over again to stroke him. All I succeeded in doing was getting bitten. Almost before I knew it February came, and the six months ended.

So one mild day we put Cookie and his cage in the back of the station wagon and drove down to the zoo. The animal keeper and my husband unloaded the cage and prodded Cookie out into the area they'd prepared for him, while I wandered about petting a baby monkey that had the run of the zoo. Then the three of us stood in front of Cookie's new cage, my husband and I looking sadly at one of the few animals our love had failed to tame. Cookie didn't even look up as we turned away.

Horses, Horses, Horses!

Back in the days when my husband was a struggling, relatively impoverished medical student, with seven cents in cash and a cupboard full of one can of green beans, we used to sustain ourselves by dreaming of the home we'd have after he finished medical school and went into practice. It would be in the country, we agreed, with plenty of room for the children to play, space for a big garden, and a pasture for horses—and we'd have a horse apiece.

Ten years after graduation we bought our country home. By that time our dreams had altered a bit—one or two horses would suffice. I, especially, favored the reduction in the number of horses. Somehow I had never gotten around to confessing to my husband that I'd never ridden a horse in my life. My total riding experience consisted of trying to hang onto the back of the bony old mule who pulled the plow for my father when I was a little girl. The mule's prime objective consisted of dislodging me, but since she was too lazy to buck, she usually accomplished her aims by walking under a low-hanging branch that brushed me off if I didn't happen to see it in time and dismount of my own accord.

During the three months between the time we signed the papers for our home and the day we actually moved in, we acquired our first two horses. One was a twelve-year-old mare named Sugar. My friend Jerry Lake had formerly owned her.

Sugar was one-quarter Shetland and three-quarters quarter horse. In size and color, she looked like a small pinto. Jerry told us he had trained her as a cow pony. He had also taught her to barrel race, once winning second place with her in a local rodeo.

Sugar was one of a trio of horses—Sugar, Salt, and Pepper—that had belonged to Jerry and his older brothers. Jerry told us how the three boys used to ride full tilt across the pasture, jump the horses six or eight feet down the riverbank into the water, and swim them across.

"Well, I'm certainly not going to let my children do anything that foolhardy!" I exclaimed.

He grinned. "That's what my parents said, too. I don't think they know to this day that we did it."

We pastured Sugar at our new property. About a month before we moved in, she gave birth to a little colt. Dark, except for a white star on his forehead, he was a joy to watch as he peeked impishly at us from behind his mother. We named him Spice.

From the beginning we handled and played with him. Danny was just six that spring, and sometimes Jerry's brother Martin would hold him on Spice for a few minutes.

We moved in during the last week of school. The first day, amid all the pressure of trying to arrange the furniture and a hundred other things, I suddenly realized Danny had wandered off. I looked out the window just in time to see him pull a chair up beside Sugar and use it to climb up onto her back. She stood as still as a statue until he was on and had both hands gripped tightly into her mane. Then she took him for a sedate walk around the pasture. He came back into the house positively glowing. After that he rode every hour he could manage to get outside.

When school ended, he had to share Sugar with the other children. Sometimes the horse felt that she'd made enough trips carrying youngsters about the pasture. Then she just stood still and waited for the current rider to dismount.

Gigi became an excellent rider that summer. Jerry came and taught her to ride Sugar over low jumps, and still later Martin brought over his big palomino stallion for her to ride. Though the latter horse was not as gentle as Sugar, Gigi handled him well. All her allowance went for books on horses and horsemanship, as well as riding clothes.

While Gigi and Ray learned to ride, Jimmy and Danny worked with Spice. Because of their constant handling he was always gentle. By the time Spice was two years old, Danny, the lightest of the children, was riding him for a short while almost every day. Because Jimmy took care of him, fed him, and brought him back whenever he got out of the pasture, Spice became Jimmy's horse.

By then it became plain that Spice would be smaller

119

than Sugar, but otherwise he showed none of his Shetland background. He was a beautiful horse. People frequently stopped by and asked to buy him, but Jimmy always refused to sell.

Spice continually grew smarter and harder to keep in the pasture. Almost every morning we'd find him out. One day Jimmy saw him jump over the fence, so we added another strand of wire to the top, which helped for a while. Then he started getting out again. This time we caught him crawling under the board section of the fence, so we put a strand of wire down there, too.

Still later he learned to open the gate. We had to get a lock. Even so, now and then someone would forget to secure the gate. During the night we'd hear Spice's footsteps on the walk or patio as he made his way to see if the one who forgot to lock the gate had also forgotten to shut the garage where we kept the grain. If he could find no grain, he would go on down the driveway and out to graze beside the road. Sometimes he held the gate open long enough for Sugar to get out, too. At least then we had an easier time getting them back inside, for if someone led Sugar back, Spice would follow.

Christmas soon approached, and I became busy every minute, taking classwork at the college and cooking for my Christmas boxes. The Christmas supper for the clinic employees and their families, for which I did the cooking, neared too rapidly for my liking.

One evening I neglected to watch a pan of peanut brittle cooking on the stove, with the result that it caught on fire and ruined my stove and one bank of cupboards. The workmen came to make new cupboards and put them in, leaving everything in an awful clutter. I went to bed exhausted. When my husband awakened me just before midnight to ask if I'd heard a noise, I mumbled sleepily that I hadn't, and that what he'd heard probably was the furnace going on.

Half an hour later the steady and violent ringing of the doorbell woke me up again. Struggling into a robe, I went to the door and opened it, to face one of our less-well-known neighbors.

"Do you have a brown horse with a white star on his face?" he demanded.

"Yes," I answered, wondering what mischief Spice had gotten into.

"My wife just ran into him and killed him about half an hour ago," he stated flatly.

"Oh, no!" I gasped. "Was—was your wife hurt?"

"No," he replied. "Only half scared to death, and her new car is totally ruined."

"I'll get my husband up," I said. "We'll have to call the sheriff or state patrol or whoever investigates these things." I started away, then turned back. "Did he suffer, or was it quick?"

"He died instantly," the neighbor answered in a softer tone than he'd been using. "And I've already called the sheriff, so someone will come here right away."

Soon I watched the lights of the cars and the flashlights as the men looked over the scene of the accident. While my husband talked to the sheriff and state patrolman, I sat and watched and shed tears for the beautiful little horse that had been clever enough to open the gate but not smart enough to stay out of the road.

Jimmy mourned for his pet, too, but it was not until the following summer that we got another pony to take Spice's place.

In the spring we began to see notices of a Central Union Bible Camp and pack trip to take place in the Little Big

Horn Mountains in August. Gigi and Donnie both wanted to go. The more they talked about it, the more interested I became. Finally I called the conference office to see if I, too, was eligible to go. They told me I'd be most welcome, especially if I'd act as camp nurse. I went up and paid the required deposit for the three of us.

Gigi spoke several times of taking Sugar on the pack trip, since the rates were much lower if the camper furnished his own horse, but we decided against it since we didn't have a regular horse trailer.

"Now, Mother," Gigi announced one day, "you're just going to have to learn to ride. We've tried for three years to get you to ride Sugar, and you wouldn't. Now you have to learn!"

"Oh," I said airily, "we have plenty of time for that. After all, what is there to riding except mounting the horse, staying on until you get to where you're going, and then getting off?"

"But how do you plan to make your horse go where he's supposed to?" Gigi asked.

"Well, surely he'll be smart enough to follow the one in front of him," I countered.

"What if they put you at the head of the line?"

"Nobody would put a person who's never ridden before at the head of the line."

Donnie grinned, and Gigi said in a tone of disgust, "Oh, Mother-r-r!"

But to tell the truth, I didn't feel nearly as confident as I tried to sound. I knew I really ought to practice *some,* at least. One day when I thought nobody was around, I went out and got on Sugar. At once the children came from every direction, each one trying to tell me what to do next.

"Now everybody wait a minute," I said firmly. "I just got

up here to practice getting on, and now I'm going to practice getting off, and I'll practice riding some other time." Then I dismounted. The children plainly showed their disappointment, and I felt I'd evaded another crisis.

I vowed to myself that before I got on Sugar again, I'd already know how to ride. I would not—absolutely *would not*—make an utter fool of myself in front of a bunch of children, including four teen-agers, even if the teen-agers were my own. So, secretly, the next day I called a riding school in town to make arrangements for lessons. They told me to call back the next day when the instructor would be there, but the next day was Sabbath, so I kept putting it off. And the next thing I knew, vacation time arrived. Telling myself that I would have plenty of time after that to learn to ride, I breathed a little easier at having a three-week reprieve from my problem.

One of our first vacation stops was a lovely state park in southern Missouri. Immediately after we set the tent up, the children ran off to the riding stables and came back to say that it had half-price riding rates in effect because of the holiday weekend. Gigi and Danny went back and signed up for the next ride. A few minutes later they rode out on the trail. When it came time for the ride to end, we went to the stable to see them return.

My husband read the schedule of rides. Turning to me, he said, "Honey, you really ought to take one of these rides. You're going to have to get some experience in sometime before that pack trip."

"I'll go if you will," I said, quite certain that would finish his bright idea.

"You won't go under any other conditions?" he asked.

"Nope!"

"All right," he sighed, walking over to the reservation

123

counter where he signed the whole family up for the three-hour moonlight ride.

Thus a couple of hours later I found myself being given an assist to mount one of the biggest, most wicked-looking horses I'd ever seen. From my perch I looked down at the wrangler adjusting the stirrups and said shakily, "But I've never ridden before!"

"Shucks, ma'am, nothin' to it a'tall," he drawled. "You're already in the saddle. All you have to do is stay there till the ride's over and it's time to get off."

I threw a grin Gigi's direction, and she looked disgusted again.

The ride began, and fifteen minutes later I started to relax. It didn't seem bad at all. Old Red—his name was on the saddle blanket—seemed to shrink until I no longer sat twelve feet above the ground. Now he seemed only a little bit bigger than the horses before and after him. Beginning to feel a stirring of affection for such a noble beast, I reached out to give him a pat on the neck. Then just in time I looked up to see the horse ahead of us break into a run. The next thing I knew, Red followed his lead. From that moment on, the only part of my anatomy in constant contact with the saddle was the one hand desperately gripping the saddle horn. Part of the time I hung onto the saddle horn with both hands and wished I were an octopus.

From one end of the line to the other, a teen-aged girl patrolled constantly, her job to keep the horses moving smartly. It seemed to me she spent a disproportionate amount of her time inciting Red to run. It got so that whenever she came in sight, I'd begin pleading with the horse.

"Look, Red, here comes that vicious child again. Step it up just a little bit, won't you? Not enough to run—just enough to keep her from hitting you with her stick."

But in vain. Red would mosey along until all at once I'd hear directly behind us, "Hiya, Red, get moving along there. Go on, you old lazybones!" The stick would whack down on Red's hindquarters, he would lunge forward, and I'd grab frantically for anything that offered a shred of security.

Now and then a member of my family would call out, "How are you doing, Mom?" If the horses happened to be walking at that moment, I'd sing out, "Doing fine. I'm still in the saddle." If the horses ran, I didn't say anything.

All things eventually come to an end, even three hours of riding a bad-tempered horse that stands skyscraper high. No lights ever looked so welcome as that first glimpse of those in the stable as we came in sight of them. They must have looked good to Red, too, for he put on an unexpected burst of speed that stopped only when he entered the corral, but I, with both my arms around his neck, still perched in the saddle.

The next day my husband complained bitterly about his legs being sore. I still felt fine. "How does it happen that you're not sore and I am?" he griped.

"The only thing I can figure out is that it's the saddle that makes you sore," I answered. "Actually I didn't spend much time *in* the saddle. I was up above it most of the time."

Luckily for me, we never stopped at any other places where we'd have an opportunity to ride, but when vacation ended, I still faced the choice of either learning to ride or else figuring out some way of going on a horse pack trip without ever actually getting on a horse.

The canceling of the pack trip due to circumstances beyond the control of our conference and union leaders settled my problem, however. I was sorry the others had to be disappointed, but as for myself, I drew my first completely easy breath since the day they had said that I could go on the trip.

Nip 'n' Tuck

"Oh, no—please, not that chair," I gasped in dismay as the somewhat obese insurance salesman started to lower himself into the inviting overstuffed chair on my sun porch.

Some of my panic must have communicated itself to him, for by dint of heroic effort he managed to hoist himself upright before his well-padded posterior made contact with the cushion.

Embarrassed at treating a guest in such a fashion and

feeling that it called for some explanation, I stammered, "You see, that chair belongs to a squirrel."

At that, his eyebrows rose to meet his hairline, and I knew I had more explaining to do. "Well, not really," I floundered on. "The chair *actually* belongs to my mother-in-law." I realized I was getting in deeper and deeper, for his expression said plainly that I was just the type to have a squirrel for a mother-in-law.

Stopping, I gulped, "I'll get you another chair," and fled. A few minutes later, after coming back with the promised chair, I felt more composed, but the salesman seemed rather deflated. He made a halfhearted effort to interest me in an insurance policy, appeared undismayed at his lack of success, and seemed only to want to escape from a place where a man had to give up his chair because it belonged—unbelievable, absolutely unbelievable!

But it was true. That chair did, for all practical purposes, belong to my pet flying squirrel. My son Ray had given them to me for Christmas, a pair of them—beautiful little animals. They had bright, dark eyes and soft silky fur, darker above than below.

They delighted me, for they reminded me of the wild flying squirrels that used to come into our house during my girlhood in the Ozarks. On summer nights the wild ones would venture in and glide about from the rafters to the furniture. We loved to watch them, for they brought with them all the enchantment of the nocturnal woods.

I named my new pets Nip and Tuck. Nip was an aggressive fellow, not at all adverse to biting the hand that fed him. Tuck, on the contrary, was a docile little thing, wanting only to curl her fluffy tail over her face and sleep in the nest of shredded paper she and Nip had piled in one corner of the cage. Perhaps Tuck's gentleness resulted not so much from a good disposition as the apathy of illness, for three weeks after Christmas she died.

Shortly afterward, Nip escaped from his cage into the larger world of the sun porch. I immediately concocted plans to get him back inside. Leaving him without food for about twenty-four hours, I then tied a string to the cage door, ran it through a couple of eyes, and secured the other end to a peanut in such a way that when Nip tried to run away with the nut, he'd shut the door right in front of his own nose and get caught again.

I went to bed, secure in the knowledge that I would find Nip safely in his cage when I got up the next morning. The next day I discovered only the shell of the peanut, still tied to the string. Too hungry to try to run away with the peanut, he'd just eaten it right on the spot. None of the other plans I made for Nip's capture worked, either, so I had to reconcile myself to letting him run loose.

Before long I found out he'd taken refuge in the aforementioned chair. Each evening I left food and water out for him, and the next morning I swept up the nut shells where he'd eaten. Sometimes when we came home late at night, we'd spy Nip high up on the tops of the bamboo drapes, his big bright eyes alert as he started the day we were just ending.

One night some odd noises awakened me—a loud "PLOP," followed by a succession of softer "plops." I crept out of bed and into the hall. There it came again. "PLOP—plop—plop—plop!" I was sure no burglar ever made such noises. The next time I heard it, I could tell it came from the sun porch. Turning on the light, I caught Nip right in the middle of a frolic. I sat down on the couch to watch.

Nip would scamper up the drapes, glide the length of the long room, and land with the loud "PLOP" I'd heard.

Then, with a series of stiff-legged little bouncing hops—the lesser "plops"—he'd bound to the drapes and scamper up, to begin all over again.

Many nights I got up to watch Nip play. Sometimes he'd let me join in by playing peekaboo with me. I'd see him peeking at me over the arm of the couch. I'd point a finger at him, whereupon he'd disappear, only to show up a few seconds later at the other end of the couch. He enjoyed it so much, I'm sure that if he'd been a human child, he would have giggled and shouted with laughter.

After tiring of his peekaboo game, he'd go gliding from the top of the drapes. Now and then he'd stop and rest a tiny paw on the toe of my slipper. I thought he was trying to coax me into joining that game, too, but I had no way of explaining to him that what was so easy and enjoyable for him was an utter impossibility for me.

One morning I found Nip's food untouched. It was still there the next day. Beginning to look for him, I nearly took his chair apart and searched the sun porch from one end to the other. All I found was a partly opened window. That convinced me that Nip had made his way into the soft summer darkness outside the window. I hoped he'd adapt quickly to the wild, find a mate, and live to a ripe old age. With his abilities, I felt sure he had a good chance to do just that.

The Lettuce Eaters

When I was about five years old, my father went away on a visit to his parents. When he came back, he brought me two pretty white rabbits. He let me play with them for a while, then he shut them up in the chicken house until he could find time to build them a hutch. Under no circumstances, he explained to me, should I open the chicken house door, for the rabbits would get out and run away.

I was the picture of patience until about nine o'clock the

next morning. Then I went out to try to get a glimpse of the rabbits. Not tall enough to look through the windows of the chicken house and at the moment still much aware of my father's admonition not to open the door, I roamed about disconsolately.

Suddenly I had a bright idea. The reason I couldn't let the rabbits out was because they'd run away, daddy had said. Well, if I made a fence so that they couldn't get away, surely nobody would mind my taking them out.

So I went to work. I made my fence, a ring of rocks, none over five inches in height, but each one carefully touching the ones next to it. When I finished it, I surveyed it proudly. That ought to hold them, I said to myself.

While I tugged and tried to open the chicken house door, the deathblow to my plans appeared in the person of my mother. I suppose I'd been quiet too long, and she had come to investigate.

"Are you trying to let those rabbits out?" she demanded.

"I want to play with them," I explained. "See, I made a fence so they can't get away."

"But that ring of rocks wouldn't hold them," she said. "They'd jump over that the first thing."

Bitter disappointment washed through me. All my work and planning for nothing! I began to cry. Mother tried to comfort me. "Daddy will make a cage for the rabbits, and then you can see them," she said.

That made me angry. I knew better—daddy had had all last night and all that morning to make a cage, and he hadn't done it. He'd just gone to the field and plowed. I threw myself down on the ground and began to kick and scream. My mother scooped me up, still kicking and screaming, and took me into the house, where I probably got the spanking I so richly deserved.

131

It is odd—I don't remember another thing about those rabbits. Though I surely must have done so, I don't remember ever seeing or playing with them again.

Several times during my growing-up years I tried to raise baby cottontail rabbits, but never succeeded. My father told me they were exceptionally hard to raise in captivity, so I gave up. Not until I married and had children of my own did I try again.

One Sunday morning in early spring I answered the doorbell to find a tall young fellow from our neighborhood standing on my front steps. Several neighborhood children struggled to look into the cardboard box he clutched chest high. My own children joined the group.

"Good morning, Bill," I said. "Won't you come in?"

"I'm sorry; I can't," he replied. "I have to be at work in a little while, but—hey, let go," he said to one of the youngsters pulling at his arm, trying to drag the box down so that he could see into it. "You'll get to see in here in a minute," he continued to the child, "if Mrs. Norman will let you."

"Bill," I asked, "what *do* you have in that box?"

"Little rabbits," he replied. "I took them away from some kids that were going to kill them. Everybody says you like animals. I didn't know what else to do with them, so I brought them here."

"Let me see," I requested.

He lowered the box. Four little cottontail rabbits huddled inside it.

"I don't know, Bill," I said doubtfully. "I've never been able to raise a cottontail yet."

"But I don't know what to do with them," he said helplessly. "I couldn't let those kids just kill them."

"Of course you couldn't," I agreed. Taking pity on his

dejection, I added, "I'll try to raise them, but I'm not optimistic about it."

He flashed me a grateful smile and hurried off to his job.

I held the box down where all the children could see and admire the little animals, but warned them not to touch them. Then I sent them all out to play, except Gigi, who wanted to stay behind.

One of the little animals already showed signs of trouble, so I placed it in a separate box and put them all in my bedroom. "I have to go to the store and get some doll bottles to feed the little rabbits with," I told Gigi. "You may look at them, but you must not touch them or take them outdoors. If they got away from you, a dog would likely get them."

Thirty minutes later I came into the yard, and the first thing I saw was a dejected little girl standing inside a ring of stones, clutching one little cottontail rabbit.

"What happened, Gigi?" I asked.

"I—I made a pen and put them in it," she quavered, "and they ran away. I couldn't catch the others." She held out the remaining rabbit mutely.

Tears of suppressed laughter filled my eyes as I remembered another five-year-old girl who tried that same trick twenty-five years before.

Gigi eyed me uneasily, wondering what punishment I had in store for her. I knew she deserved it, but probably she'd learned her lesson. Besides, I argued with myself, she didn't kick and scream the way I did when I got caught, and that ought to count for something.

"Come on in," I said. "We'll have to feed this fellow."

The sole surviving rabbit—the sick one had died during my trip to the store—learned quickly to drink from the bottle and surprised me by never faltering in his march toward maturity. When weaned from his bottle, he learned to eat rabbit food. He outgrew his box and one day got loose in my bedroom. Since we had never handled him much, we couldn't consider him tame. He was just a wild rabbit living in our house.

During the day he took refuge under a big upholstered chair in the bedroom. Each evening I put out food and water for him before I went to bed. We kept a tiny night-light in the room in case I had to get up to see about the children during the night. Sometimes I'd awaken and see the rabbit eating and drinking. He made no sound as he hopped about, but if I moved, he would scoot back under his chair in a flash.

Toward fall he had grown so much that he had a hard time crawling under his chair. We decided it was time to turn him loose. I thought he would be better able to take care of himself than if we had made a pet of him. He wasn't easy to catch, but finally I cornered him in the closet, and throwing a towel over him, I carried him outside.

When I set him down, he never hesitated but raced away as if his life depended on it. Perhaps it did.

Several years went by before we had another rabbit. One Easter my husband brought home a tiny white bunny, which we christened with the unlikely name of Apple Blossom because of the pretty pink skin inside his ears. From the beginning we adored him as we have loved few other pets. He seemed to thrive on being held and played with. He ate and grew and ate and grew until he was an enormous rabbit, nearly as big as our dog and far more fierce. I had never heard a rabbit growl before, but Apple Blossom growled. The sound was soft and throaty, but what it lacked in volume it made up for in sincerity—no one could mistake the menace in it.

Apple Blossom had a broad streak of jealousy in his

makeup, mostly directed toward the dog. We made use of it when we wanted to catch the rabbit. Sometimes we'd let Apple Blossom outside to play on the lawn. He loved that, all the room to run in and all the fresh grass and clover he could eat. The only problem was, when the time arrived to come in, Apple Blossom wanted to stay out longer. When we went to pick him up, he didn't run away—he just loped easily a few steps ahead of us, even pausing now and then to snatch a bit of grass or clover.

Finally we worked out a way to get Apple Blossom every time. Two of us would take the dog out and begin petting her. As soon as Apple Blossom saw that, he'd come running as fast as he could, growling at the dog. One of us would pick up the dog, and the other would pick up the rabbit; otherwise, Apple Blossom would struggle to get down if we left the dog down on the grass.

That rabbit never showed the least fear of anything. If a strange dog came in the yard, Apple Blossom would growl and try to get out to battle with the intruder. I think he would have attacked an elephant if one had ever wandered in.

We'd had Apple Blossom more than a year the day Jimmy came running up from the basement, screaming at the top of his lungs. I met him at the top of the steps. With tears streaming down his face, he showed me deep scratches on his bare legs and arms.

"Apple Blossom!" he sobbed. "Apple Blossom did it!"

I realized that, painful as the scratches were, the knowledge that Apple Blossom, his dearly loved pet, had attacked him hurt even worse.

"I went down to feed him," he went on, "and he knocked the dish out of my hand and——"

I shuddered, thinking of our habit of holding Apple Blossom up in front of our faces as we talked to him, or of burying our faces in his fluffy white fur. I was deeply grateful that he had not chosen such a time to use his claws.

"Don't cry, Jimmy," I said. "I've read somewhere that some rabbits get that way, but Apple Blossom has always been so sweet and gentle before that I never dreamed he'd act like this."

"What are we going to do with him, Mamma?" he asked.

"Well, we can't have him run loose in the house anymore," I answered. "We'll have to put him outside in a cage. Isn't there a big cage out by the garage?"

"I think so."

Raymond walked in at this point in our conversation. "What happened to Jimmy's legs?" he asked.

"Apple Blossom did it," Jimmy said.

"Apple Blossom?" Ray said unbelievingly. "You must have hurt him or something, Jim."

"No, I didn't," Jimmy denied. "I just went down there to feed him and——"

"I'll go down there and see for myself," Raymond interrupted, and he hurried down the basement steps before I could stop him. He raced back up much faster. "I see what you mean, Jim," he said. "He came after me, too."

"Let's get him into that big cage out there by the garage," I said. "He's too dangerous to remain loose any longer."

Apple Blossom didn't like the cage, but we told him it was his own fault. We put in some old rags for a bed, and fed and watered him faithfully, keeping out of reach of his claws. One of the rags making up Apple Blossom's bed was an old jacket. One day in the middle of summer he tried to crawl into the jacket sleeve, and suffocated. We buried him at the corner of our lawn where we had put the bodies of several of our other faithful pets, and chose to remember him as he was when still sweet and loving.

136

Tiki

I'm glad I answered the phone when it awakened me that morning, for it led to an experience that I wouldn't have missed for more money than it cost me.

"Mrs. Norman, this is Tim Gregg," said the voice on the line. "Do you remember me?"

Too sleepy to be tactful, I muttered groggily, "I don't think I do."

"I'm the man with the ocelot," he explained.

"Oh, of course," I replied. "I guess I always think of you that way instead of by name."

"The reason I called, I know a man who has one for sale cheap. Since you've always been so interested in our Tabu, I thought of you right away. He wants only $60 for it. Do you want it?"

Wide awake by now, I said, "It sounds good. Tell me more about it."

"Well," Mr. Gregg said, "it is about a year old. He was born in a zoo in Iowa—Des Moines, I believe. A woman here in town bought him and made a pet of him, but she had to go to work, so she sold him. His name is Tiki, by the way. Anyway, she felt she couldn't give him all the companionship he needed if she had to be gone all day. A man I know bought him and put him in the same cage with another, and Tiki killed the other one the same night."

"You mean he didn't give them any time to get acquainted before he put them in together?" I asked, astonished that anyone handling animals would ignore such a fundamental rule.

"No, he didn't. He says he knows it was a mistake, but it's too late now. He was quite fond of the other ocelot, so he just wants to get Tiki out of his sight as soon as he can. He's been looking for a buyer for almost a month now."

"Well, I'd be glad to take him," I said. "How big is he? I'd better know that before I commit myself too deeply."

"He's about the size of Tabu," Gregg answered. "About fifteen to twenty pounds, I imagine."

"Nearly full-grown, wouldn't he be, at a year?" I questioned.

"Just about. Maybe grow a little bigger, but not much."

"All right, then I'll take him," I said. "Now, if you'll tell me where to go after him——" I paused.

"I might make a suggestion—perhaps it would be wise to have his fangs and claws removed before you bring him home," Mr. Gregg said. "We had that done for Tabu. I don't think ocelots are safe without having this done. Even Tabu, as tame and gentle as she is, might hurt someone if she were frightened or even just playing."

"That is a good idea," I concurred. "I wouldn't have thought of it myself."

"If you'd like, I'll go and get the animal Sunday night and take him down to the animal hospital Monday morning for his surgery," the man on the telephone offered. "Then you can pick him up there and bring him home while he's still under the anesthetic."

I accepted his offer. Monday morning when I got to the animal hospital, they had already put Tiki under the anesthetic. He was a beautiful animal, even spread-eagled on the surgical table.

Mr. Gregg gave me a list of the things I should get—a special leather harness called martingale, a litter box, water dish, etc. Oh, yes—chicken necks for food.

After every errand I stopped to see how work progressed on Tiki. At home I got the big wire pen with the hinged lid, in which we'd kept a few guinea fowl the preceding summer. It was just the right size for Tiki. I placed the pen in the living room on a big scatter rug—I wanted Tiki to get used to us from the beginning. After padding the bottom with newspapers and a blanket, I fastened a piece of plastic around the corner of the pen where I would put the litter box, for Mr. Gregg had warned me that ocelots have a tendency to spray.

Then I packaged twenty pounds of chicken necks into twenty one-pound containers and stashed them in the freezer.

Now, what else? Oh, yes—the martingale. Mr. Gregg said we should put it on while Tiki was still asleep. But, unable to find a martingale, I had to settle for less. The last purchase consisted of a book on ocelots.

Late in the afternoon I brought Tiki home, all four paws thickly bandaged and a bit of bloody saliva trickling from his mouth where the hospital had removed his fangs. The veterinarian and Mr. Gregg had both given me advice on Tiki's care. The doctor reminded me to be sure to turn Tiki every two hours until he awakened to prevent pneumonia. Mr. Gregg said I should pet and talk to the animal so that as it recovered it would get used to my touch and the sound of my voice, but I should, above all, not get my face down close to it, even if I felt sure it was asleep. Both warned me that Tiki might rouse from the anesthetic rather suddenly and spring at me, so I must be careful.

That night I got up faithfully every two hours to turn Tiki. Each time I found one or another of the children checking him. By morning two of the children had fallen asleep on the living-room couch and another on the floor next to the cage.

Tiki slept all day Tuesday. I turned him and moistened his mouth with water every two hours. By evening he would pull his paws away if I touched them. The ocelot book said that indicated returning consciousness. Wednesday he opened his eyes and drank. I held him and talked to him much of the day. During the night he got up and moved across the cage to the litter box. He ate and drank by himself. By Thursday noon he snarled viciously every time I came near. No more petting. Fortunately we had put on the harness and removed the bandages from his feet before he awakened.

I received plenty of good advice from every side as to the taming of my new acquisition. At last I mapped out my own strategy. First Tiki must learn to take food from my hand. Then he must come to me for food. After that—well, after that it would be only a matter of time until he learned to trust me.

Three weeks went by. Tiki still snarled each time I came near him. Every day I spent whatever time I could spare sitting beside the cage and talking to him. My husband began to fear that Tiki might get out and hurt me, and began suggesting that we donate him to the zoo. Personally, I still felt that, given enough time, I could tame Tiki, but after listening to my husband's hints about the zoo, I began to suspect that I was now fighting a losing battle on both sides.

Then a young man from the pest control service offered to buy Tiki. He was new on the route, and it being his first call at our house, he didn't know ahead of time about our collection of animals. But he knew animals.

"An ocelot!" he exclaimed. "What a beauty! You—you wouldn't be interested in selling him, would you?"

"Oh, I might," I answered.

"How much do you want for him?" he asked eagerly.

I named a price that, after paying for Tiki's surgery, would leave me a profit of almost ten dollars.

"You really mean it? You'll sell him to me for that?" he asked again.

"Yes, I really will," I assured him.

"All right. I'd like to take him today." He paused a moment. "I guess if we're going to do business together, I'd better introduce myself. I'm Brent Barker. I came here from California last June to attend dental school, and I'm just waiting to see if they'll accept me or not." He had a charming smile.

"I'm glad to meet you, Brent," I said. "As long as you're

141

going to be with the pest control service, we'll be seeing you now and then anyway."

"Next month you will, but after that I'm being moved into the front office. They've promised me a job on the sales force."

"Sounds good," I commented.

"Sounds good to me, too." He smiled. "First time I've ever been on my own two feet, and I had to leave home to do it."

"Did you say you were from California?" I asked.

"Yes, Fresno. My dad—my adopted dad—was city attorney there for many years. He was always so good to me and so ready to give me all the money or anything else I ever wanted, I had to get away to see if I could make it on my own."

"We have two adopted sons," I said.

"You do? Wonderful! My parents were killed when I was nine years old, and the Barkers, close friends of my parents, took me in. They are Catholic, and I'm Jewish, but they never tried to change me one bit. After my Bar Mitzvah at thirteen I let them adopt me."

"They sound like wonderful people."

"They are. They really are!" Brent said sincerely. "They were just too good to me. Why, when I was just a little kid, they let me keep a boa constrictor for a pet. He was the gentlest thing. We named him Alexander. All the kids in the neighborhood used to come, and we'd carry him around the block—it took seven or eight of us to do it. Sometimes that snake and I would play together in the yard. I'd turn the hose on him, and he'd hit at it with his head and pretend he was going to knock it out of my hand. Finally he got so big we had to get rid of him. We gave him to a zoo. I used to go visit him now and then, but he always recognized me and tried so hard to get out of his cage that they asked me not to come anymore. I surely missed him. I've always loved animals.

"Now about this ocelot. I could write you a check for the full amount right now, but if you'd trust me until the first of the month, you'd be doing me a great favor. You see, I'm buying some General Electric shares through a deal where they automatically deduct the money from my checking account. If I write you a check and the other comes due at the same time, and there isn't enough to cover the check for the stock, they will cancel my whole deal. I'll lose all the money I've put in."

"Well, I——" I began, having had little part in the one-sided conversation for some time.

"The reason I want the ocelot now is because I'm buying him for my fiancée," Brent broke in. "I promised her something special, meaning to get a greyhound—I used to raise champion Dobermans in California—but I know she'd like an ocelot better. If you could let me have him now, I'll pay you in full the first of next month. My job should be security enough; you know the company I work for, and they've promised me a promotion."

"I think we can do business on those terms," I said, "but if you want to take Tiki today, you'll have to wait until my husband comes home to help get him out of the cage. He should be here within an hour."

While we waited for my husband, I listened as Brent outlined his plans for taming Tiki—essentially the same as I'd hoped to use.

"And I've the perfect place for him to stretch out," Brent said enthusiastically. "I've a shaggy white rug I'll spread on the mantel above the fireplace. It's warm, and I'll bet he'll love it."

143

"I imagine he will," I agreed. "They like high places."

"I'll have to move my bar," Brent mused. "I keep my drinks on the mantel. I don't drink, myself, except for an occasional beer, but I keep the fixings on hand for my friends when they visit me."

"What will your landlord say about Tiki?" I inquired.

"Oh, I have the grandest landlord. His name is Mr. Sawyer. He told me I could have any kind of pet I wanted so long as it was quiet. I always ask if the management will allow pets before I move into an apartment."

About that time my husband came home and heard that I had sold Tiki. I thought he seemed unduly pleased.

Nearly two hours later, Tiki, sound asleep from a sedative I'd injected, was on his way to his new home. Nearly a month went by. I wondered at times how Brent was getting along with Tiki, but knowing he would come around for the pest control service soon, I didn't bother to call him.

Then one day I drove into the driveway and saw the pest control service truck parked by the garage. "Good!" I said to myself. "Now I can get my money and see how Tiki is!"

But the serviceman was not Brent. It was the man who had had the route before Brent came.

"Where's Brent?" I asked. "Did he get that promotion sooner than he expected?"

"You mean Barker?" the man said. "He got fired nearly a month ago for laziness and general incompetence!"

"But—but he—bought an ocelot from me," I stammered.

"And never paid you for it, I'll bet," the man interjected.

"No! No, he didn't!" I said. "And I was considering his job as security."

"Well, you won't likely get your money or the ocelot back."

"I know where he lives," I persisted. "I will, too, get that ocelot back."

The man shook his head slowly. "He's moved," he said. "Nobody knows where he is now. I'll tell the boss about this, and he'll help you all he can, but I think you've just lost your animal."

After the serviceman had gone, I sat dejectedly facing the fact that a pro had swindled me. Then a slowly growing anger and determination not to let the episode end like that took hold of me. I *would* get either my money or the ocelot back, or at least give it a good try.

My husband came home shortly and listened to my story. He shook his head. "Forget it, hon," he advised. "You don't have a chance to get Tiki back!" I knew he hoped he was right.

"I will. I will, too!" But I only thought it to myself—I didn't say it aloud.

The next morning I made phone calls and phone calls. I contacted the zoo, the Humane Society, and all the veterinarians I knew, telling my story and leaving Brent's description so that they could notify me if he showed up or tried to dispose of the ocelot.

Then I called my lawyer, who poked gentle fun at me for letting myself get swindled, and told me he didn't see what we could do if nobody knew where Brent was. He inferred that it would be best for me to forget the whole thing and chalk it up to experience. That, I was not willing to do. Finally he said he'd give the matter further thought.

That evening I got in touch with Brent's landlady. I told her my story. She told me hers. They had never given Brent permission to have a pet of any kind, but one day about a month before he had told them his father was sending him an unusual cat from California. Thinking it was some kind of domestic cat they told him it would be all right for him to keep it. Then one day they discovered Tiki in Brent's apartment and asked Brent to move because of it. Brent refused to leave. Finally they had to get a court order to evict him. He had moved only two days before, leaving no forwarding address, and taking several of the things that belonged to the apartment, including the telephone.

"Did he take the ocelot?" I inquired.

"Yes, he did," she replied. "He wasn't good to that animal at all. Sometimes he'd be gone for three days at a time and leave the cat without food or water. We were afraid of it, so we couldn't feed it."

The woman and I promised each other that we'd keep in touch. If either of us located Brent, we'd let the other know.

The next morning I talked with Tom, my husband's business manager. He had had years of experience in tracing people. "Let's try the credit bureau first," he suggested.

After the call he turned to me and said, "The boy has a wife named Judi. They don't know the whereabouts of either. They'll send a full report by mail."

"But—but he said he bought the ocelot for his fiancée," I sputtered. "If he's married, isn't that misrepresentation or fraud?"

"Could be," Tom answered.

"I'll talk to my lawyer again," I said.

But the lawyer advised me to notify the police. I decided to wait until I had the full credit report on Brent.

Two days later I sat in Tom's office as he read it. Then the phone calls began again. Former landlords, business acquaintances, every lead on the paper told us the same story. Brent Barker was a smooth talker, incorrigible liar, and a writer of bad checks. He stole money when he could, property if someone left it unattended, and so far had managed to keep ahead of the law. Everybody was sympathetic, nobody knew where he was, and everybody wanted to know.

The last reference was a company with no local listing, its regional headquarters in a city fifty miles away. "No use calling that place," I mused. "Let's keep the calls local and save the expense."

"It won't cost much," Tom said calmly, and proceeded to place the call. He asked for the personnel manager of the company. I could hear only a tantalizing half of the conversation that went on and on. Tom's portion went, "We are trying to get some information about a young man named Brent Barker. He . . . yes, I know he doesn't, but . . . no, not a bad check. He defrauded . . . oh, you, too? . . . What's that? . . . Three years old? . . . Back in June? . . . I see. . . . A telephone? . . . Oh! . . . You don't know where . . . Yes, of course. . . . I see. . . . Yes, we'll be glad to. You'll hear from us. Good-bye!"

"Well, Tom, what is it? What did he say?" I asked, wildly impatient to hear the rest of the conversation.

"He said," Tom recounted slowly, "just about what everyone else has had to say about Brent Barker, plus some more. He told me he fired him for dishonesty over a year ago, after Brent had cheated him out of several hundred dollars. Then he said Brent came to him last June and asked him if he'd keep his little three-year-old son——"

"Three-year-old son!" I interrupted. "Barker had a son?"

Tom nodded. "That's what the man said. Barker asked him if he'd keep the little boy overnight, and he said he would. Barker was to pick him up the next morning, but they haven't seen him since."

"That's been five months ago," I exclaimed. "What else did he say? I heard you mention a telephone."

"Yes, the personnel manager said he saw a telephone in Barker's suitcase when he unpacked the little boy's clothes."

"He took the telephone out of the Sawyers' apartment when he left there last week," I commented. "Do you suppose he has a thing about telephones? I think he's a bit psychotic myself."

"Maybe so," Tom agreed. "Barker was in trouble in California some time ago for impersonating an FBI agent, but nothing came of that. That man said the police in his city want Barker on several different charges, including child abandonment."

"Where's the baby's mother? And what is going to happen to the little fellow?" I asked.

"The parents got a divorce before Brent left California. And the man he left the little boy with is filing a suit for permanent custody. I said we'd let him know if we located Barker."

"Thanks a million, Tom," I said. "Could I have a copy of that report? It may come in handy when I go to the police this afternoon."

Just as I was leaving to go to the police station, the phone rang. One of the persons I'd contacted earlier called to say that he had the address at which Brent was supposedly living. I wrote down the apartment number and went on.

The police were polite, but apparently helpless. They called to see if Brent had left a forwarding address with the postal authorities. He hadn't. I gave them the address of the apartment. They called the caretaker of the building, who told them Brent didn't live there. It didn't surprise me. Evidently they couldn't help me, either, unless I located the culprit for them.

Back home again, I happened to remember that Brent mentioned his activities with a local theater group. In answer to my call, the woman in charge said he had left their organization ten days before. She said he'd always been close to his rabbi, but I didn't want to bother the rabbi with the problem except as a last resort.

Another day went by. Then my husband telephoned from the clinic late in the afternoon to tell me that Brent had called there and left a message.

"Did you talk to him? What did he say? Tell me!" I demanded.

"No, I didn't talk to him," my husband replied. "He left a message with the receptionist, saying he was sorry there was a misunderstanding about the ocelot and that he'd come out to see us either tonight or in the morning, and we'd talk it over."

"Misunderstanding!" I fairly exploded. "The only misunderstanding I know of is that I thought he was going to pay for Tiki! Did you get his phone number or address?"

"No," came the answer. "The receptionist asked for it, but he refused to give it."

"I wonder who told him I was hunting him," I mused.

"You can ask him that when he comes to talk tomorrow," said my husband.

"He won't come," I predicted confidently. And sure enough, he didn't.

That evening Mr. Gregg phoned and asked about Tiki. I told him the whole story. He, too, thought it was a pity I was so gullible as to let someone defraud me of my animal, but promised to help any way he could to get Tiki back. The next evening he called back. His wife worked as a hostess in one of the nicest restaurants in town. That day one of the waitresses mentioned to her that a customer had told her about his pet ocelot, how he'd had it only a month or so, and how it was getting more and more savage

149

as time went on. From the description, we felt sure it was Brent. Mrs. Gregg said that if he came in again, she'd have the waitress detain him until the police could come.

A few more days went by. Then the friend who had given me Brent's address called again. "Do you have your ocelot back yet?"

"No," I answered. "That address you have is a phony. I had the police check it, and Brent doesn't live there."

"Yes, he does," my friend insisted. "I checked up on that myself, and he's there, all right. I think he's living with some other boys. Wait a minute, and I'll give you his phone number."

I really didn't have much faith in the phone number, but I dialed it anyway. The young man who answered refused to say whether Brent Barker lived there or not, but after I told him I'd let the police handle it, he called Brent to the phone.

Acting on the theory that the best defense is a good defense, Brent began by angrily demanding to know why I had inquired about him at the theater. And where had I gotten his phone number?

I told him that I was not at liberty to reveal where I had obtained his phone number. As for his first query, I said that I was justified in using any lead available to track him down. We had done some intensive investigation, I explained, and learned quite a bit about him, which led us to believe we'd better take the ocelot back.

He remained silent. So was I for a moment. Then he said, "I'm not working right now. I lost my job. I'll have to make some arrangements and call you back tonight or early in the morning." Before I could insist that I wanted the animal, not money, he hung up.

Not having heard from him by noon the next day, I

telephoned my lawyer again. "Let's get the county attorney in on this," he suggested. "I'll call and tell him our story, and then I'll contact Barker."

A short time later he called back. "Barker is going to bring your ocelot out to you tonight. If he doesn't, let me know, and the county attorney will have a man out to pick up that young fellow first thing in the morning."

But Brent didn't bring the ocelot home that night. Before noon, though, I got a call from Brent. "Mrs. Norman," he said, "I'll bring Tiki back just as soon as the sedative takes effect. You'll be surprised at how tame I've gotten him. He eats out of my hand, and comes to me and lets me pet him."

I thought of what he'd told the waitress a few days before, but I didn't mention it. Instead, I said, "Take Tiki to the animal hospital rather than bringing him here. I want the doctor to check him over."

Two hours later I got word that Tiki was at the hospital. My husband and I talked it over and decided to give Tiki to the zoo. He had been so mistreated and was reacting so viciously that we didn't want him at home.

The zoo was happy to take him. They went down and got him before the sedation wore off. In the zoo he seems happier. There he has only to be an ocelot, not a pet or a conversation piece.

Cold-blooded Crawling Things

As a child in the Ozarks, I learned from my family and neighbors a healthy respect for copperheads, cottonmouth moccasins, and rattlesnakes; a tolerance for black snakes, rat snakes, and other harmless types; and I made playthings of the pretty little green grass snakes. We would catch the grass snakes and tie them in loose knots around the fence. They always extricated themselves from such a position, apparently none the worse off.

I heard the tales, fact and fancy mixed, that the oldsters in our area related. They told about the joint, or glass, snake, which supposedly disconnected itself into half a dozen pieces whenever something molested it. After the danger ended, the pieces would wiggle back together to become one whole snake again. Some old-timers whispered that unless you cut a snake's head off when you killed it, it wouldn't die until sundown. And then they described the hoop snake that took the end of his tail in his mouth and rolled like a hoop as he chased his victims. The spur on the end of the hoop snake's tail was supposed to be poisonous, the hill people claimed, not his fangs.

One man told an incident that involved a friend of his wife's cousin, and he knew it was true because his wife's cousin had told him so. The man was out cutting timber when he saw a hoop snake coming toward him. He had only time to dodge behind a tree, and the snake stuck its spur into the tree instead of the man. Before the snake could withdraw its spur from the tree, the woodcutter killed the snake with his ax. However, the tree had absorbed so much of the venom that it swelled and swelled and swelled. It grew so big that the man got enough lumber from the one tree to build himself a new house. When he went to paint his new home, he thinned the paint with turpentine, forgetting that turpentine would reduce the swelling, which it did. When he got through, he had not a new family house but a birdhouse.

I personally never saw a hoop snake or a joint snake or any other of the exotic species of snakes that reportedly inhabit the Ozarks. I never met anyone who did. But I have met dozens of people who had friends and relatives who knew someone who had.

As my children grew, I tried to teach them to keep their

hands off any snake they weren't sure about. At the same time I tried not to transmit my own fears to them. Like every adult I knew, I would remark, "I'm not *afraid* of snakes. I just don't like them." The truth was, I *was* afraid of snakes. Little vestiges of the old stories seemed to flicker in the corners of my mind whenever I ran onto a serpent, and even after I had identified it as harmless, I still could hardly conquer my aversion to it, for even nonpoisonous snakes can bite.

And yet, I could appreciate their beauty and sinuous grace. Whenever we visited a zoo, I never avoided the snakes, but admired the pink and brown mottling of certain constrictors, the sleek and shining scales of the ribbon snakes, and the tender green coloring of the green tree python, among others. I'm sure the glass between us made it easier to admire them.

One little girl in our neighborhood had a pet black snake. I never saw it, but one of the members of my Pathfinder unit told in shuddery glee how she'd spent a night in that home, and the snake crawling across her face had awakened her. I just shuddered.

It is likely that my feelings about snakes would have retained their *status quo* if I hadn't received an invitation to represent my conference at a youth leadership training camp down in Texas. A friend of mine would be the other delegate from our state, so we made plans for our trip. The camp offered classes of all kinds. Lula and I together signed up for campcraft, she chose a class in bird study, and I decided to take the one on mammals. We had to pass up the classes on insects, herpetology, water sports, and others. There just wasn't time enough for us to take everything offered that seemed interesting to us.

The camp was beautifully situated beside a small lake.

Lula and I stayed, along with about ten other women, in the medical cabin right next to the lakeshore.

The schedule promised to be a strenuous one from early morning until campfire was over. Those of us who took the mammalogy course had to get up earlier than the others and examine our traps to see if we had caught any specimens during the night. One bright spot in the day was the rest period scheduled for right after lunch.

Lula and I wanted very much to take the class in herpetology, and apparently a good many others did, too. At suppertime the first day the leaders announced that the instructor would teach an extra class in herpetology during the rest period for those who wanted to take it.

The next day a greater number showed up for the extra class than for the regular class. The professor had cages and glass boxes full of all kinds of snakes. After the orientation lecture, he demonstrated the handling of snakes. We all gathered around to watch.

One box had about a dozen black snakes in it. "Now, remember," he warned us, "if you put your hand in slowly where there are black snakes, you're likely to get bitten. But if you put your hand in fast, you're *sure* to get bitten!"

Slowly, and with infinite caution, he eased his hand into the box, carefully picked up one of the snakes, and brought it out.

"See," he announced triumphantly, "I didn't get bitten!"

Whereupon the snake struck suddenly and bit the man standing next to the professor!

During the next class period the professor got a big rattlesnake, a sidewinder, and put it on the ground so that we could see the way it crawled. A sturdy picnic table stood nearby. Fortunately it was strong enough to hold all the feminine members of the class who took refuge on top of it.

155

Before long the members of the class began poking about in likely places trying to start their own snake collections. One night a group decided to go up the lake in canoes and watch while the professor took some pictures of frogs. Lula and I were in the group, but because we were nonswimmers, he restricted us to the rowboat. We found a couple of men who agreed to row the boat for us, one of them being the MV secretary of our own conference. He had brought along a butterfly net with which to try to catch the big bullfrog that croaked off-key during our campfire each evening. I had a battery-operated lantern to provide the light.

By the time we got started, the others in the canoes had far outdistanced us. We never did catch up, for as we rowed along, we suddenly noticed the big water snakes down in the water. Our MV secretary decided to collect a few to take back home and show at junior camp. Lula, the nature instructor at junior camp, naturally favored the idea.

He put the butterfly net to use, and within a few minutes he handed Lula a big snake to hold. A few minutes more, and she had one in the other hand.

"I don't have any snakes," I complained. I really didn't want one, either, but I hated even worse for them to discover that I was afraid of snakes.

So I received the next snake, and neither it nor I died of fright. Soon Lula and I had two snakes in each hand, about all we could hold, and we went back to the dock. It is no easy thing to disembark from a rowboat when you have both hands full of snakes. The snakes were not easy to hold onto, either. They weren't slippery, as most people think they are; but they were strong and possessed a determination to get back to their natural habitat. One of mine got his head into my blouse pocket and tried his best to get the rest of himself in after it.

156

Lula and I walked to the door of our cabin, then discovered that neither of us could open a hand to turn the doorknob. We finally got the knob turned by using our elbows, and no sooner had we solved that problem than we faced another. Where were we going to put the snakes? We stood there, trying to keep from laughing, both well aware that if any of our cabin mates awakened and saw us standing there with our hands full of snakes, we'd have a few cases of full-fledged hysteria on our hands.

Finally, I managed, by using my teeth, to get the pillowcase off my pillow, and we crammed the snakes inside it. Then I sacrificed one of my shoestrings to tie the improvised snake sack shut, and we put it in the sink and went to bed. Sometime later we both awoke with the horrible thought, "What if someone else gets up to use the sink before we wake up in the morning?" We crept out of bed and hid the snakes under the wood in the fireplace. Early the next morning Lula took them up and put them in with the professor's snakes.

Lula and I had noticed the pretty little lizards—now green, now brown—that ran about the camp. In class we learned that they were American chameleons. The teacher also told us that we would not be able to catch any. We wanted some to take back for our junior camp and hesitated to believe that we couldn't get them. Try as we would, though, we weren't able to get our hands on one.

Then one morning I seemed to have a chance. It was during the announcement period at flag raising, and we all stood at attention. Noticing a flicker of movement on the tree beside me, I saw a chameleon sprawled across the bark. Attention or not, I intended to get that lizard. Cupping my hand, I leaned forward for the pounce that would put him in my possession, when——

"ATTENTION! WE'RE AT ATTENTION HERE!"

I jumped, the lizard fled, and I straightened up to see the camp leader looking directly at me. Ah, well! Maybe next time I wanted to catch a chameleon the camp director would be somewhere else. I hoped so.

Lula eventually caught a hog-nosed snake, I captured another water snake all by myself, and the last afternoon at camp she and I went on a hike to see if we could augment our supply of reptiles. We had a small plastic sack with us, in the unlikely event we caught a chameleon. For some reason or other—either the lizards were slow that day, or we were just quicker than usual—before we returned to our cabin, the sack contained *nine* chameleons.

That night a group of us got together with the herpetology professor for an armadillo hunt. Most of us came from regions where the armadillo does not live, and those armored-tank-type animals fascinated us.

Most of the ladies from our cabin got into the station wagon, the professor and another man perched on the hood of the car, another young man lay full length on the luggage carrier on top to man the spotlight, and with Lula at the wheel we drove slowly over little backcountry Texas roads looking for armadillos.

Whenever the man with the light spotted one, Lula would stop and the professor and his companion would jump off the hood and give chase, trying to throw their jackets over the animal and catch it. They caught no armadillos that night, but I'm sure some of the animals got the scare of their lives.

Though the evening was unsuccessful as an armadillo hunt, it was not a total loss. Once we stopped and looked at a big tarantula that appeared in the road ahead of us. Another time the spotlight caught a fox as it roamed about.

The fox stood still for a minute, silhouetted against the trees, then trotted leisurely back out of sight, the spotlight showing clearly his every move. And of course jackrabbits abounded everywhere.

We got back to our cabins at midnight for a few hours of sleep before starting for home at five in the morning.

The next morning in Dallas we picked up a woman who wanted to ride back home with us. She screamed when she saw my mammal specimens mounted on their board, yelled a little louder when she spotted the bag of chameleons, but reserved her most ear-splitting shriek for the pink pillowcase full of snakes. But she was a good sport, and aside from a fearful glance over her shoulder now and then, she did all right on the long ride home.

We were within fifty miles of home when we heard and felt the ominous "thump-bump, thump-bump" of a flat tire. We pulled over to the side of the road and looked at each other.

"What do we do now?" inquired our passenger.

"We get out and stand beside the road looking helpless, and pretty soon a man will come along and change our tire for us," I suggested.

He appeared within five minutes. The spare tire lay under the floor of the station wagon with all our luggage piled on top of it. Our passenger from Dallas had added a sewing machine, pressure cooker, and other miscellaneous items to the things Lula and I already had, so the car was full. The gentleman was helping us unload when I decided to warn him about the bag of snakes.

I shined the light in on it and said, "That pink pillowcase is full of snakes." To give support to my words, the case began to move as one of the larger snakes decided to change its position.

Our Good Samaritan gave a most unmasculine scream, jumped back about six feet, and stuttered, "When you get down to the spare tire, and take the snakes down the road a piece, call me and I'll change your tire."

While he changed the tire, we told him who we were and where we had been. He kept exclaiming, "I've met lots of people in my life, but I never ran into anything like this before. Nobody's gonna believe this when I tell it. Never thought I'd meet *women* with snakes in their car. This is a real education for me."

We offered him money, which he refused, saying he wouldn't have missed the experience for anything. I thought, since we had contributed to his general knowledge and given him conversational topic for several weeks to come, perhaps we were even. Lula wasn't content to leave it at that. She felt he deserved a reward of some kind, so she decided to show him her prize snake, the Texas hognose. When she brought it out, you could tell that his feet wanted to run, but his pride wouldn't let him. Having felt that way quite often myself, I quickly recognized it in others.

He listened to Lula's lecture on snakes, declined her offer to let him hold it, and in general kept his composure pretty well. Finally he managed to break away, waved us a happy good-bye, and drove off.

The snakes were great hits at junior camp that summer. Lula taught her class in herpetology, and the children loved it. The big status symbol at camp was to be able to display the marks of a snakebite. Each evening at campfire the camp newspaper listed the names of the campers who had been bitten during the day. And the biggest mystery at camp was why the nurse and the nature instructor would be looking at the snakes, and suddenly, for no reason anybody could see, go off into spasms of giggles.